Nigerian
Folk Tales

As told by
Olawale Idewu and
Omotayo Adu

Second Edition

Archon Books/1980

Nigerian Folk Tales

Edited by
Barbara K. and
Warren S. Walker

Text Decorations by Margaret Barbour

Library of Congress Cataloging in Publication Data

Nigerian folk tales as told by Olawale Idewu and Omotayo Adu

I. Walker, Barbara K.   II. Walker, Warren S.
III. Idewu, Olawale   IV. Adu, Omotayo
V. Title

GR351.3.N53   1980   398.2'09669   80-10771
ISBN 0-208-01839-5

© Barbara K. and Warren S. Walker 1980
First edition published 1961 by Rutgers University Press. Second edition first
published 1980 as an Archon Book, an imprint of The Shoe String Press, Inc.,
Hamden, Connecticut 06514

For Frances and Bill Rutter

Acknowledgments

We wish to make grateful acknowledgment of assistance rendered to us by the following people: Dr. Kirk Strong, for material helpful in understanding the fertility tales; the Blackburn College Language Laboratory staff, chiefly Sandra Eden, for the use of recording facilities; numerous librarians, especially Mary Ambler and Homer Lee Sutton, for locating elusive pieces of scholarship; and Dr. Herbert Halpert, for his kindly counsel on bibliography.

A Note on the Decorations

The text decorations, which are based upon photos of actual Nigerian art objects, were reproduced from linoleum block prints designed, cut, and printed by Margaret Barbour. The small spot ornaments, also linoleum cuts, were adapted from decorative features found on these and other Nigerian artifacts.

The artist and authors are indebted to the Segy Gallery for African Art in New York for the use of the photographs from which the drawings on the half-title and title pages and chapter headings for "*Pourquoi* Stories" and "Trickster Tales" were taken; to the Carlebach Gallery, New York, for the photograph used for "Demon Lovers"; to Olawale Idewu for his photograph of the bird in the collection of Dr. Lorenzo Dow Turner of Roosevelt University, Chicago, used for "Moral Fables"; and to Gordon Fikejs for his photograph of the statuette in the collection of the authors, used for "Fertility Tales."

vii

Contents

CONTENTS

Nigerian
Folk Tales

Introduction
to the Second Edition

The time appears ripe for a second edition of *Nigerian Folk Tales*, a volume intended to bridge the gap between wholly undocumented collections of Yoruba tales and the scholarly studies published within the past two decades in Nigeria, in the United Kingdom, and in the United States. Our purpose is to whet the appetites of readers for further exploration of Yoruba verbal art at either or both ends of the spectrum of its publication. Guides for such exploration are provided in this Introduction, in the Supplementary Notes, and in the expanded and updated Bibliography. Apart from the original bibliography, the first edition is furnished intact herein; it has not lost its pertinence despite the flood of publications succeeding Nigeria's attainment of independence. We are of course well aware that the Yoruba constitute only one of the three major ethnic groups in Nigeria and that in that respect the title appears too broad for the content. The other two major ethnic groups—the Ibo and the Hausa—are represented by references both in this Introduction and in the Bibliography; readers are encouraged to supplement the present handful with samples from collections and studies of Hausa and Ibo folktales in order to arrive at a fuller understanding and appreciation of "Nigerian" oral narrative.

In the preparation of the second edition of *Nigerian Folk Tales*, we have benefited greatly from the comments and counsel of a number of Africanists, chief among them William Bascom, Daniel Crowley, and Bernth Lindfors, and we wish here to acknowledge that indebtedness. We wish also to note three errors our mentors detected in the first edition: In "The Lion, the Tortoise, and the Boar," "Boar" should be "Boa," and "Boar" should likewise be "Boa" in "The Tortoise and the Boar"; also, "her" should replace "his" in the last sentence of the original note (p. 000) for "The Elephant and the Tortoise" since the author whose work is cited is female.

In the Supplementary Notes we have discussed Yoruba variants of eighteen narratives selected from *Nigerian Folk Tales*, drawing some of the variants from collections or studies prior to 1961 and others from volumes published since the appearance of *Nigerian Folk Tales*. All variants considered in the Supplementary Notes were chosen from works listed in the Bibliography. The similarities and differences noted between the variants and the forms in which the tales were told by Olawale Idewu and Omotayo Adu evidence the degree of innovation permitted to and encouraged in Yoruba storytellers. The uses and abuses of this freedom to innovate can be appreciated most fully after reading the entire texts of the variants cited. Whether the differences must be attributed to "acculturation" or to considerations of translation and/or style seems to us a less central matter than the fact that such differences do characterize the handlings of any story strong enough to endure in the Yoruba oral tradition.

Both the tonal feature of the indigenous language (whether Ibo or Yoruba) and the non-Western sentence structure appear to pose decided problems in the translation of Nigerian folk narratives. For helpful insight into sound translation of Yoruba texts, see Bascom's two-step technique in his *Ifa Divination, passim;* for instances of content-and-style translation from the Ibo (Igbo), see Thomas's *Anthropological Report on the Ibo-Speaking Peoples of Nigeria*, Volume 3, Part 3, *passim*. The all-too-common assumption that Yoruba tales are "simple" and "plain" has been based largely on retellings or adaptations or summaries done by those unaware of the drama, art, and language play inherent in the indigenous-tongue originals. With the current dedication of the Yoruba themselves to the preservation and valid presentation of Yoruba verbal art, we may well come to a fuller appreciation of the richness of this viable narrative tradition.

A number of heartening developments—largely since 1960—have encouraged in-depth investigation, analysis, and publication of Yoruba tales. Not least of these is the determination of the Yoruba themselves to preserve these carriers of values and traditions. The universities in southwestern Nigeria have established academic programs devoted to the language and literature (both oral and written) of the homeland; the results of this emphasis have been apparent in popular and scholarly journals, in papers read at national and international professional conferences, and in books of enduring worth published in Yoruba and/or in one or more Western languages.

Further, a lively awareness of the potential loss of indigenous oral art—especially in urban areas deprived of traditional storytelling milieux—has prompted primary-school administrators and leaders in various mass-media enterprises to include Yoruba legends, folktales, and proverbs in the school curricula and as attractive regular features on the radio and on television. (The broadcasts are offered in English—the present lingua franca in Nigeria—and at intervals in the vernacular, to maintain respect for and familiarity with the indigenous tongue.) Thus radio, television, and formal schooling—which in many countries have displaced the instruction and entertainment afforded by the storyteller—have become tools in strengthening the ties of the Nigerians (the Hausa and the Ibo as well as the Yoruba) with their ethnic traditions. The Ibo, not to be outdone, are rapidly expanding the preservation of their own verbal arts; the Society for Promoting Igbo Language and Culture has been especially effective in this effort.

In addition, the increased field use of recording equipment both by Nigerians in situ and by contemporary non-Yoruba collectors of verbal art has facilitated the preservation of the tone, mood, mimicry, and audience response associated with a well-told folktale. Sterile summaries, telescoped tellings shorn of the songs integral to the originals, and precious adaptations of Yoruba tales will gradually be recognized as the gross misrepresentations of genuine Yoruba narration that they have always been, and convincing recreations of these lively tales will eventually supplant those earlier collections and studies unable to evidence their continued worth. Itayemi and Gurrey, in the Introduction to their *Folk Tales and Fables,* specify with regret the alterations that mark the " 'Englished' " volumes of Yoruba tales, including their own (pp. 11–12); an awareness of these alterations should be helpful to readers in evaluating the printed materials currently available, especially those listed in the Bibliography, in terms of the degree to which the tales have been restyled to suit the authors and have thus lost the distinctive flavor of the originals.

Further encouraging developments on both the Nigerian and the Western scenes include the vastly expanded publication of Africa-related books by a mushrooming body of publishers, the greatly increased participation of university faculty and students in Africa-related seminars and symposia, the flood of new journals and professional organizations devoted to African issues and literatures, the burgeoning of African studies programs in colleges and universities in the United Kingdom and in the United States, and the reprinting of many Africa-centered books far too long unavailable to readers. The development of archives of African verbal art has drawn both interest and funding; also, a significant number of African students continuing their studies abroad have collaborated readily with non-African specialists in African verbal art, both on articles and on books. (Note, for example, the study of Yoruba proverbs by Bernth Lindfors and Oyekan Owomoyela.)

A giant step has been taken, too, in the reassessment of the type and motif indexes long used to identify African as well as European and New World folktale elements. These indexes, ill suited to the analysis of African tales, have been supplemented—beginning with Klipple's "African Tales with European Analogues" (1938), a valuable link between the old and the new—by several useful and pertinent works (unfortunately, as dissertations not yet published, but available in xerographic form). Chief among these works are Clarke's "A Motif-Index of the Folktales of Culture Area V—West Africa" (1958), Arewa's "A Classification of the Folktales of the Northern East African Cattle Area by Types" (1966), and Lambrecht's "A Tale Type Index for Central Africa" (1967). (A recent volume evidencing the pertinence of the newest indexes for studies of African oral narrative is Ross and Walker's *"On Another Day . . .": Tales Told Among the Nkundo of Zaïre*, in which citations are drawn from all six indexes, clearly identified.) Another dissertation *not* an index but entirely relevant to the present study is LaPin's "Story, Medium and Masque: The Idea and Art of Yoruba Storytelling," a three-volume work indispensable for assessing the care and dedication with which today's investigations of African oral narrative are being undertaken.

African studies appear at last to have assumed their rightful place among the academic disciplines. It seems increasingly important for *non*-academic readers to gain at least some acquaintance with this new and better-informed look at Africa. We trust that the second edition of *Nigerian Folk Tales* will encourage such readers to explore both the present samplings and those suggested in the Bibliography, and to reassess their own assumptions concerning the strength and savor of African folktales and the varied cultures out of which those tales have grown.

Barbara K. and Warren S. Walker
Lubbock, Texas

Introduction

Prior to our time the folk tale was for Nigerian audiences what it has always been for unlettered groups: the only means of transmitting a native culture. Legends, beliefs, mores, and social attitudes descended from one generation to another largely through the medium of the folk tale, that most functional form of what William Bascom has called "verbal art." But contrary to the effect produced in so many underdeveloped areas, the oral tradition did not lose its force with the coming of the British to Nigeria and the advent of the written word. Despite a growing system of formal education, and despite a marked increase in the literacy rate, the oral tradition is still very strong in the country today. Some observers interpret this as a conscious resistance to the process of acculturation: the oral tradition, excluded from the school curricula and frowned upon by missionaries, has become a kind of "underground" expression supporting the new nationalism surging through the land. Cultural anthropologists tend to discount such a theory and attribute the survival of these tales to other factors, chiefly the appeal of their indigenous humor and satire and the skill of the native storytelling. Whatever the causes, there is clearly a great residuum of native Nigerian culture at a time when, on the surface, the country is rapidly acquiring Western habits and manners.

I

All of the tales in this volume came from the extensive repertoires of Olawale Idewu and Omotayo Adu, two Nigerian students at the time pursuing their education in this country. Both come from Yoruba families still influenced strongly by the oral tradition, and both men are excellent raconteurs after the fashion of tale-telling in their culture.

Olawale Idewu, who told us most of these stories, is a Christian convert presently preparing for the medical profession. He was born in Abeokuta, Western Nigeria, the home of his mother and her parents; now, most of his family is living in Lagos, the federal capital, which was the home of Mr. Idewu's father and of his paternal grandparents. Both of Olawale Idewu's grandparents were chiefs, one in Abeokuta and the other in Lagos. One of the streets in Lagos bears his grandfather's name, "Idewu Olo" ("Idewu the Youth," since there were two Idewus in Lagos in his day and he was the younger-looking one). Ola heard these folk tales from the adult members of his family during the period between his seventh and sixteenth birthdays.

Omotayo Adu, a Moslem, had lived all his life in Lagos (where both his maternal and paternal grandparents also lived), until he came to the United States to take undergraduate and graduate work in chemistry. His father died some years ago, and his mother (one of three wives of his father) has supported her children comfortably in Lagos. The tales Mr. Adu told us were heard during his childhood from members of his family and from other adults in the neighborhood in which he lived. Much of the ethical teaching which he received came through the telling of didactic tales such as those included under "Moralistic Tales" in this collection.

The differences in their backgrounds illustrate somewhat the cultural diversity of the Yoruba people. Although all of southwest Nigeria is now classified for political purposes as Yoruba territory, it is only because the Yorubas are the dominant tribe in the area. Only about half of the 8,000,000 people living there derive originally from Yoruba stock; the rest are descended from numerous other tribes, among them the once prominent Egbas and the Benis. Idewu's Abeokuta was once the capital of the Egba tribe, and Ibadan, the seat of Nigeria's first university, was an Egba settlement; Benin was the center of the Benis, a tribe long distinguished by its fine craftsmanship and art work. Farther north in Yorubaland are people of Hausa and Fulani origin, both Moslem tribes whose religion has been adopted by many Yorubas, Adu's family included in the number. Emerging as the political and cultural leaders of western Nigeria in the eighteenth century, the Yorubas have now fairly well assimilated most of the other tribes in the area. That theirs is the official native language west of the Niger River is but the most obvious token of this pre-eminence.

II

For the Yorubas the telling of tales is a leisure-time activity, occurring after supper, when relaxation is sought. The young male adults gather on a doorstep in the moonlight, and one of the group initiates the session by asking two or three riddles. This practice ensures that the circle will be wakeful and alert, a precaution deemed necessary in a society where folk tales are always at least partly didactic in purpose. Such riddles as these may be posed:

Q. What god requires a sacrifice of every man, woman, and child three times a day?

A. The throat [or the belly], because it must have food three times a day.

Q. What is it that dares to knock the king on the head?

A. The knife, because the king must shave.

Q. What is it that goes past the palace and does not greet the king?

A. The stream, because it flows past the palace speaking to no one.

Many of the riddles, of course, involve word play and therefore suffer in translation.

Storytelling among the Yorubas, as among a number of other African peoples, is a dramatic and musical performance, as well as an oral one. Narrators identify themselves quite thoroughly with the characters in their tales, imitating with appropriate movement and gesture the action described. So strong is this dramatic tradition that on a number of occasions our informants themselves, carried away by their material, imitated the actions of various characters. Mr. Idewu, for example, in describing the desperate effort of the hunter to secure the alligator in "The Hunter Who Was King," dug the air vigorously with his imaginary cutlass, quite earnest in the pursuit of his elusive prey, and forgetful of the impersonal microphone before him and of the alien setting of an American living room. And Mr. Adu, in telling of the attempt to entice the elephant-king to the village (in "The Elephant and the Tortoise"), half prostrated himself, even as the tortoise indicated respect for the ruler-elect.

In several of the stories he told, Mr. Adu spontaneously

sang the verses sung by the characters in the tales, moving
to the Yoruba tongue for these interludes. The tonal intervals in these songs are much smaller than can be approached by the notes of a standard piano, and the musical
effect is both haunting and curiously appropriate to the
mood and content of the tales. The interchange of songs
between the small bird and the tortoise in "The Elephant
and the Tortoise" lends an immediacy to the action and an
intensification of the elephant's perplexity and indecision.
And in "The Girl Who Knew the King" the repeated mes-
sages sung by the helpful parrot utilize music effectively to
impress upon the listeners a tale strong in social impli-
cations.

On many occasions the listeners in a Yoruba storytelling
circle may themselves participate in the performance.
Sometimes they sing the choruses; sometimes they beat
drums and play other instruments to heighten the effect of
the story. And at the conclusion of an especially fine ren-
dition, they may indicate their appreciation of the art of
the performer by cheering.

The highest appreciation of the storyteller's art, however, will be measured by its influence upon the behavior
of the listeners. And it is to achieve this moralistic end
that all possible artistic means are employed—movement,
gesture, songs, accompaniment, and changes in tempo and
pitch of voice.

III

Perhaps the most distinctive feature of this volume, from
an ethnological point of view, is the way in which it illustrates the alteration of traditional tales to fit the demands
of a changing cultural situation. In some instances this

produces distortions of older narratives, several of these so pronounced that they lead to mutations in plot development or theme.

Some of these distortions are conscious ones, alterations intended to make the narrative more acceptable or intelligible to a non-African listener. For example, in the first story, the senior wife would "set a table"; and the new wife "would abandon her bed and sleep on the floor"; she would "desert her chair to sit on the floor, and . . . refuse to eat with her husband and the other wife." These observations, readily appreciated by an English or American listener, bear no relation to the actual cultural setting of the story. Traditionally, wives in a polygynous society occupied separate huts, so the senior wife would have had no opportunity of observing the new wife's sleeping practices. Also, sleeping mats on the floor customarily served as beds; and tables were not used. And it was not permitted to wives to eat with their husbands. Acquaintance with Western cultural patterns allowed the teller thus to adapt a domestic situation which might otherwise be perplexing to his American listener. (Other interesting conscious distortions will be cited in the notes for individual tales.)

Unconscious distortions—ascribed perhaps to the narrators' extended absence from Nigeria, their growing familiarity with a non-African written tradition, and their own skill in improvisation—also appear. One cultural mutation of this sort allows the telescoping of a long dramatic narrative into the present form of "The Hunter and the Witch." This abbreviation is accomplished by the introduction of a comment that would not occur in a traditional rendering of the tale: "It is a wonder that, despite the hunter's skill in native charms and allied magic, he could not detect that the woman was a witch." (Such skepticism about the powers of hunters would normally violate the common view of their role in the Yoruba cultural milieu.) But by this device the teller sets the scene for the action to follow, without including several incidents apparently present in the version told at home. Divergencies of this kind do not, however, exceed the artistic license permitted accomplished storytellers.

It is interesting to note that the extent of distortion is greater in the tales told by Mr. Idewu than in those told by Mr. Adu. The difference can probably be attributed to their religious backgrounds. Islam has traditionally been less zealous in the rooting out of native lore in the areas it has entered than has Christianity.

IV

There are different ways in which the material of such a volume as this can be arranged. We have grouped the tales, as much as possible, according to the Thompson Index of types. Throughout the four tales of the first section, Demon Lovers, runs the theme of mixed marriages between mortals and otherworldly creatures of various kinds. The Why-Stories or *Pourquois* of the next section, parallels to which can be found in every primitive society, illustrate folk efforts to explain among themselves the nature of things in the physical world. So strong is the moralizing tendency in all forms of Nigerian folklore that the third group, Moralistic Tales, may not seem to merit a special section. These, however, are fables, many of them reminiscent of Aesop, which exist *solely* for the moral; they are brief, direct, and always overtly didactic. In the next section, the escapades of Tricksters, by contrast, entertain as much as they teach, for the listener enjoys the ingenuity through which the protagonist succeeds. The tales of the last section, like those of the first, are marked by a single theme: the difficulties women sometimes have in conceiving children. Fertility is the key to social status for Nigerian women, both within the frequently polygamous families and beyond that in the community at large. So carried away are the Yorubas by their preoccupation with fertility that in their tales even men sometimes become pregnant!

There has been little attempt to edit these tales in such matters as form and style, or to change them in any way, except for making the pronoun *he* refer always to the male character and *she* to the female. (In Yoruba there is no distinction in speech to indicate gender, and our two narrators have a tendency to use *he* and *she* interchangeably.) Although several of the tales might benefit, from a *literary* point of view, by reorganization or even rewriting, such temptations were forgone.

The tales are taken almost entirely verbatim from oral renditions. They were collected over a period of five years, at first during visits that our informants made to our home and later during planned sessions at our college offices and at the Blackburn College Language Laboratory. As the two men gradually became accustomed to working with modern equipment, they were willing to record their tales for us, and most of the stories that appear in this volume are transcriptions from magnetic tape.

Perhaps a word should be said about the language of the tales. The English idiom may strike one, at times, as impossibly literate for material that 1) has been transmitted orally, and 2) is quite foreign to the culture patterns of the Anglo-American world. This effect is partly the result of translation: neither informant had ever heard the tales told in English, and both were translating from the Yoruba even as they narrated. The literary quality derives also, in part, from the formal rhetoric taught in British colonial schools, a rhetoric whose balance and stateliness echo the prose style of the eighteenth century. One suspects, too, that such proverbial expressions as "Paddle your own canoe" and "You have made your bed and you have to lie on it" are only rough English equivalents of Yoruba locutions. In the process of their thus "Englishing" the tales, undoubtedly the tellers have lost some of the original flavor.

Tales of

Demon Lovers

 The Hunter and the Deer

Far away and long ago in a small village there was a youth who was gentle by birth but a hunter by necessity. This youth was the most handsome man in his village, and he was very famous because he had never come home empty-handed. His fame coupled with his handsomeness made him the idol of the whole village.

One day he went to a nearby forest to hunt. It was his habit to climb a tree and watch for his quarry. But this time, though he stayed in the tree for hours watching, he could get no animals. It was about time to go home. The sun was already on the horizon and darkness was fast approaching. He decided to climb down and set out for home.

All of a sudden, he saw a deer. As he was aiming an arrow against the deer, he saw it begin to remove its skin. Greatly amazed, he kept on watching. The next thing he saw was a very beautiful woman. He continued watching. And this woman quietly and carefully hid the skin under a stone near the tree in which the hunter was watching.

The hunter observed all that went on, but he did not say anything. The woman went away. After the woman had disappeared, the hunter came down, went to the stone and lifted it up, and took the deer skin. He examined it carefully. Then he put it in his satchel and went home.

On the following morning the hunter took his satchel containing the deer skin, slung it on his shoulder, took his bow and arrows, and made for the forest. As he had done the previous day, he climbed the tree. But this time he was looking for the reappearance of the beautiful woman, as well as for quarry. After several hours he had seen nothing but a snake, which unfortunately escaped before he could capture it.

It was sunset, and time for him to go home. As he was starting to come down again, he saw the woman coming toward the stone. The hunter remained quietly in the tree, watching what would happen. The woman lifted up the stone to recover the deer skin, but she couldn't find it. She was very much worried. She ran helter-skelter. She beat herself, cursed herself, and was very much anxious. The hunter, who had all the while been watching her, called suddenly, "What are you looking for?"

The woman said, "Oh, I was looking for the deer skin which I hid here yesterday."

The hunter asked, "What would you do for me if I could get you the deer skin?"

But the anxiety of the woman to get the deer skin overshadowed the idea that the hunter could help. What she was doing was just to be searching under the trees and in nearby caves—wherever she could think to look.

The hunter called again, "Don't you think I could help you to get the deer skin?"

Then the woman looked up and saw the hunter. Although she was afraid, the anxiety to get the skin drowned her fear, and she replied, "If you could get me the deer skin, I could get you anything you want."

The hunter said, "I will give you the deer skin if only you will promise to be my wife."

With a smile on her face, and a little blush, the woman answered, "How can I be your wife? I cannot. Just give me my skin if you have found it."

"Well," said the hunter, "since you are not willing to do anything to reward me for finding the skin for you, I'm not prepared to give it to you."

At length the woman agreed to be the hunter's wife on one condition: that he would tell no one what he had observed. The hunter took an oath of secrecy, and promised not to reveal the secret to any human being. And the woman was satisfied. Since she had promised to marry, she thought she would have no need for the deer skin, for she did not wish to change into a deer again. But the hunter kept the skin in his satchel.

Well, the hunter and the woman went home. On their entering the village, they were met by all the neighbors, who were very curious about this beautiful woman. When they inquired about her, the hunter told them that he had met her in the nearby town where he went to hunt.

Before this time, the hunter had married a wife. His wife, aware that the hunter would soon be home, had the house clean and the table set for his arrival. To her amazement, she saw her husband enter with another woman. She questioned her husband: "What about this woman?"

The husband replied that he had met the woman in a nearby town, and the king of that town had said he should marry the woman. He therefore had no choice, and he had to bring her home. His wife couldn't do otherwise than to welcome this new woman. And the woman was really very beautiful. Well, they would carry on.

But this new wife, despite her being beautiful, began to show some traits which could not be reconciled with human behavior. At times when the senior wife would set a table, this woman would choose to eat directly with her mouth from the plate, either sipping the soup or lapping it. This caused the senior wife to wonder what kind of woman this was. She tried to persuade her husband to tell her more about the woman, because she was surely not merely a human being. But the husband refused to say anything, because he was afraid to tell his wife the story of the transformation. And not only that—he was afraid of breaking his promise.

The senior wife left the case as it was, but this new wife continued her peculiarities. At times she would abandon her bed and sleep on the floor. Many times she would desert her chair to sit on the floor, and at times she would refuse to eat with her husband and the other wife. Then, when everybody else had gone to sleep, she would go down at midnight to the kitchen to enjoy alone the remnants of food in the pots and pans.

Again the senior wife, noticing all these things, asked her husband to tell her more about the woman, but the husband again refused. He kept telling her, "I know you love me, but I cannot tell you more than what I have already told you, because I have told you the truth."

The senior wife, still greatly worried, consulted one of

14

her friends about the problem. And that friend advised her to try to give her husband an alcoholic drink so that he would become intoxicated. Under the influence of alcohol he would surely reveal the secret.

The wife kept to herself what she had learned from her friend. On the very next day she set the table and gave a very good meal to her husband. The new wife was away, drawing water for the household. When the hunter was drunk, his first wife asked him again, "My beloved husband, couldn't you tell me more about this woman? I am interested."

The hunter then related the whole story. He told his wife how he had seen this woman transforming from a deer into a beautiful woman, how she had come the next day to look for the deer skin, how he had made a promise to her, and so on. And he told her also that he had hidden the deer skin in the attic. Many times he had gone to the attic to see the deer skin and thought of destroying it. But each time he had left it there, because he feared what effect it would have on him to destroy the magic skin. So he had kept it for a long time. When he had finished the story, his wife said nothing.

On the following morning the hunter went to the nearby bush to hunt. He would return in the evening. While he was away, the senior wife was preparing some dishes, and the new wife was helping her. Accidentally the new wife put sugar instead of salt into the soup. The senior wife spoke sharply. "Look, no matter how long you live with human beings, you never seem to leave your animal behavior."

"What do you mean?" the new wife asked, puzzled.

The senior wife replied, "I'm just trying to tell you that you should behave as a human being, and you should leave your animal behavior."

The new wife, greatly annoyed, challenged the senior wife to fight. And the senior wife, beside herself with rage, ran to the attic and got the deer skin. She flung it into the woman's face and said, "Well, I shall be very glad to miss you in this house."

The beautiful woman, greatly angered, rushed at the senior wife and killed her. Then she went into her room with the deer skin, changed to a deer again, and ran into the bush. In the bush she found the hunter. As the hunter was aiming at the deer, the deer said, "Behold, do not shoot at me. I confided in you, but you have betrayed my confidence. You have made your bed and you have to lie on it. Go home and see what has happened. I trusted you, but my love you denied."

The hunter, wondering what the deer could mean, was greatly amazed. He could do nothing but go home. On reaching home, he could find neither his first wife nor his new one. But before his arrival in the village, the news of what had happened had taken wing, and almost everybody in the village had heard what had happened in the hunter's house. So his neighbors told him what had happened while he was away.

He was so sad and so lonely that he thought himself useless, and wished that he had died as a child. He cursed himself and regretted what he had done.

Because he had told his neighbors lies, they hated him. The hunter lost his fame, and everybody turned against him. He was hopeless. Life became uninteresting. And this once-famous hunter died in agony, and uncared for.

The inference in this story is that we should be contented with whatever we have. This hunter was not contented with one wife. He wanted to have another one. And in getting the other one, he lost both.

The Hunter and the Witch

After a long wandering, wearisome, and fruitless day of hunting, a hunter strode desperately to a nearby village. In this village there was a festivity of some kind. At this festival there was an exceptionally beautiful young woman surrounded by young men of respectable personality. This small but distinguished group arrested the hunter's attention.

He drew near to see what was going on. He noticed that these men, in turn, were trying to throw "ege" [tree seeds used as marbles by children] into the woman's calabash [a gourd used for making bowls and other utensils]. After inquiring about, he learned that the woman had promised to marry any man who could successfully throw the "ege" into the calabash from a specified distance. Every one of the young men had tried and failed.

The hunter decided to try his luck. After all, the reward would be worth his trouble, and it would offer some compensation for his unfruitful hunting. There were three pieces of "ege" to be thrown. He threw the first one, which landed directly in the calabash. His second throw was successful, and so was his third. The hunter automatically became the husband of the beautiful young woman, much to the envy of his competitors.

The hunter, not knowing what type of woman he had taken for a wife, gladly took her home. It was a wonder that, despite the hunter's skill in native charms and allied magic, he could not detect that the woman was a witch who had decided to come to that town when she was bloodthirsty.

This hunter had three dogs who served as his body-guards. The bride, not noticing that these dogs were watching her, changed at midnight into a big mass of teeth. As she prepared to start her regular bloody task of chewing the hunter, his three dogs barked loudly, and the man awoke. His eyes were heavy. He sleepily asked his wife what was going on.

"Nothing," she replied. "The dogs must be either dreaming or rabid." And the hunter went to sleep again.

Thrice this woman tried, and thrice did these dogs bark vehemently to waken the hunter. The day dawned, and found the woman still unsuccessful. But she hit upon an expedient. She would go a-hunting with him and advise him to chain down his dogs, who might be a menace to his life since they appeared to be rabid.

The hunter, as a bird runs to the snare, chained his dogs, and took along with him his new wife, to go a-hunting in a lonely forest. A few hours of walking took them to the heart of a very thick, secluded jungle where no sound pervaded the atmosphere. "Whatever power you have, be prepared to use it, for you are going to die," the woman declared. She then changed to a mass of teeth, as before, to chew the hunter.

The hunter, aware of the danger, quickly climbed a nearby tree. The mass of teeth started to bite the tree to fell it. As the tree was about to fall, the hunter recited a magical incantation and another nearby tree bent to pick him up. This mass of teeth felled every tree that picked him up until the hunter was on the last tree in the jungle. There he was, on the last tree, with the mass of teeth busy at the base of the tree to fell it. There was no other hope at all; his dogs were chained at home.

Suddenly the hunter caught a glimpse of a bird flying toward his house. He called the bird, and implored him to go to his house and unchain his three dogs. By magical chants the hunter conjured his dogs to the scene before his wife—who was come from nowhere—could fell the last tree. He commanded the dogs to kill her.

In the twinkling of an eye one of the dogs had done the job. The second lapped the blood, while the third cleaned up the spot. The hunter climbed down and returned home unhurt with his three dogs.

 ## The Hunter Who Was King

Once there was a hunter who was very poor and unfortunate. Unable to get enough to eat, he was desperate almost to the point of taking his own life.

So he went to consult a *babalawo,* a diviner, who was believed to be able to tell a man's fortune. And this diviner advised him to go out and try to hunt, and to be satisfied with whatever he found, no matter how small or unworthy it might appear.

Early the next morning the hunter set forth into the bush with his gun and his cutlass. After quite a time of looking around, he saw an alligator. Remembering what the diviner had told him, he determined to get the alligator, even though at another time he would have thought the alligator a poor quarry. He resolved not to let this alligator get away, and he pursued it closely. But the alligator at last made his escape into a hole in the ground.

Since the alligator was the last hope of the hunter, he could see nothing to do but to dig down into the hole after it. So he laid down his gun and began to dig in the hole with his cutlass, to recover the alligator.

He felt his feet sinking down into the hole, and the next thing he knew he was in a town where there was no man. This town was occupied entirely by women. And since there was no man, the head of that town was a woman, who was queen.

On this day there was some kind of ceremony in the town. The hunter was amazed, and he stood and watched. After a few minutes, as he stood, the women became aware of his presence and diverted their attention to him. He was no more surprised to see them than they were to see him. The hunter had never seen a town where there had been no man. And the women had never seen a man before.

The women of the town extended their affection to him. They took him in, and invited him to stay with them. And the queen was so amazed to see him that she commanded her servants to make room for him in her palace.

On and on this man was happy in the town, and everything was going along well. As time went on, the queen developed an interest in him, and they fell in love. And the hunter and the queen married. Automatically he became the king of the town.

The queen took him through the palace, and she said, "Everything that is in this palace belongs to you, and everything in this town. There is only one place that you are not permitted to go." She took him to the door of a certain room in the palace. "You may go everywhere in the palace, everywhere in the town, but in this room. This one room you must not enter."

"Well," said the king, "that is perfectly all right. With all the other rooms for mine, and all the town, it would be strange if I were not satisfied."

And for a long time he was satisfied. He had everything to make him happy—fine food, a fine palace, a good

20

many servants. He had been poor, and now he was rich. He began to think that he was all in all and could do whatever he pleased.

So one day the king sat down and began to think. "After all, I am the king. All the palace belongs to me, with everything that is in it. All the town is mine. All the children are mine. What is there in this town that I cannot see if I want to see it?"

And sneakingly one day, when the queen was away, he went to the door of the room he was not permitted to enter. He opened the door and stepped through.

The next thing he knew, he was standing just where he had stood before when he had hunted the alligator. There was his gun. And there was his cutlass, still by the hole. But the queen, the palace, the town—all these were gone. And he was poor again. He was sorry for what he had done, but it was too late.

The hunter returned to his village and sought out the diviner who had helped him. He told the diviner all that had happened. "Help me," he pleaded. "All that was mine, and I have it no longer. Tell me how I can return to that town where I was king."

The diviner shook his head. "You had your chance, and now you have lost it. I warned you to be contented with whatever you found, but you were not. There is nothing I can do to help you."

So this hunter, once a king, with all at his command and everything to make him happy, was become once more a poor hunter.

The moral is this: We should be contented with what we have, and when we are told not to do something we should try not to do it. We should not feel too important to be within the law.

The Wolf-Prince

In a small town there lived a man who had a very remarkably beautiful daughter. This girl was old enough to marry, and many eligible suitors had appeared, but the father had not found any of them worthy to become his daughter's husband. So beautiful was this girl that many respectable gentlemen, including nobles and princes from distant places, vied with one another to win her. And so adamant was the father that the rivals became disgusted and resolved to refrain from chasing a wild goose.

The daughter and her mother were not happy at the situation and complained bitterly against the father's meticulousness. The complaint against this selective father became so intolerable that he decided to go to the "Aristocrats' Fair" to seek a suitable husband for his daughter. And he secretly took a solemn oath before Opa, their god, that the first living thing he came across at the Fair should be his daughter's husband. Forgetful of the influence this oath might have on his hopes, the father promised his wife and his daughter that from the Fair he would bring an ideal husband, one well worthy of marrying his only daughter.

The father had told only one person, his closest friend, of the oath he had taken before Opa. But among the daughter's rejected suitors was the nephew of this close friend, and he soon learned about the oath. The nephew, a fine young prince, resolved to win the bride. Disguising himself in wolf's clothing, he went to the Fair very early.

On that same morning, the father also went very early

to the Fair, to be sure that he would have a fine choice of husbands for his daughter. And the father and the suitor in wolf's clothing, being the first two at the Fair, soon met each other. So the "first living thing" the father came across at the Fair was the wolf. What a surprise! He moaned under his breath, "What a calamity!"

He had taken an oath and he must stand by it. Opa was ubiquitous; he knew everything; he could do anything. And the penalty for the breach of an oath was a shameful death. There was no choice, therefore, but for the father to take the wolf to the daughter as the promised ideal husband.

The daughter and her mother were gorgeously dressed, waiting for the promised husband. What was their horror to find out at last that the husband was no prince or noble, but a lowly beast! The daughter was in a most unfortunate dilemma. She could either take the wolf as her husband or be disowned by her family. At length, through the persuasion of her parents, the beautiful girl agreed to go with the wolf as his life partner.

On their way to the jungle for their honeymoon, the wolf removed his wolf skin and showed himself to be the handsome prince who had proposed to marry the girl. And instead of going to the jungle, they went to a luxurious palace. So happy were the couple and their parents, who had received a blessing in disguise.

Pourquoi Stories

 Why the Sky Is So Far Away

Centuries ago, when eyes were on knees—instead of their present position—the sky was so low that it could be touched by any person of average height. Men at this time could communicate with God in heaven. There was happiness everywhere. Holy men paid occasional visits to God in His glory and majesty.

So abundant was food and so luxurious was life that most of the people began to forget themselves and to neglect God's nearness. So defiant the people became that God was annoyed with them, and He poured out of heaven an unusual rain which turned everybody that came under it into a leper. As a result, most of the people became lepers.

Disgusted with their condition, hopeless and helpless, they became desperate. Instead of praying to God and giving thanks after every meal, these lepers would stretch their deformed hands toward heaven and clean them against the sky, making it their napkin.

Offended at their action, God moved with the sky far away from them—beyond their reach. Since then, the sky has been infinitely far from man.

 ## Why the Bat Comes Out Only at Night

In days gone by, there was a war between the birds and the animals. The bat, not knowing which side to take, did not at first join either side.

When he saw that victory was leaning to the side of the birds, he flew to the birds to join them. One of the birds, seeing him, asked what business he had in their camp. "Don't you know that I am one of you? See my wings," the bat declared. Finally he was accepted by the birds.

But unfortunately for the birds, the victory swayed to the side of the animals. The bat deserted the birds and went over to the animals. One of the animals, who had noticed him in the camp of the birds, demanded, "What are you doing here? Are you a spy?"

The bat replied, "I am one of you. Can't you see my teeth?" And the bat parted his lips to show his small teeth.

The animals refused to accept him, and the birds refused to have him back. Since that time, the bat has remained a social outcast. And so complete was that isolation that the bat even today does not go out from his home except at night.

The Hand and the Fingers

The five fingers are brothers. Why, then, should the thumb be isolated from the rest of his brothers? The isolation is his own choice.

It happened one day that their parents were not at home, and the youngest of them, the small finger, told his brothers that he was hungry. The third finger appealed to the hungry brother to be patient till their mother could return.

"Let us go to the neighbor's farm and get something to eat," the second finger suggested.

"Suppose the owner of the farm should see us? What would happen then?" queried the first finger.

"I had better keep my distance," said the thumb. And ever since that time, the fingers and the thumb have been isolated from one another.

 ## Why the Tortoise's Shell Is Cracked and Crooked

A long time ago there was a famine in a certain small town, and there was nothing for anybody to eat. All the young people of the town gathered together to deliberate on their problem and to determine what might be done to mend matters.

And at length they all agreed to kill and eat their old people, since that appeared to be the last resort. So everybody killed his mother except Dog, who was very clever.

Instead of killing his mother, Dog took her to heaven, where there was enough to eat and to spare. Any time that Dog was hungry, he would go to a secluded grove and sing:

> Oh, loving Mother,
> All the animals kill their mothers,
> But Dog is wiser
> And saves his mother.
> Send down your rope
> To carry me in hope
> To eat out of your abundance.

His mother would then send down a rope which Dog would hold to carry him to heaven. After his meal in heaven, the same rope would let him down on earth again.

Meanwhile, all the others had eaten their mothers, and that source of food was gone. They became emaciated and ill-looking. But Dog was fat, fresh, and good-looking. Everybody was curious and puzzled about Dog's exceptionally good condition. Every one of the animals asked Dog how he managed to maintain such a fine physique, but he refused to tell the truth. He would only say, "That's just the way it is. That's my constitution."

But Tortoise was not satisfied with this answer. "I shall find out about this," he decided. One day, after watching Dog closely, Tortoise was successful in following his footprints to the secluded spot where he was accustomed to going. Hiding himself nearby, Tortoise listened to Dog's song, and observed the rope that descended to receive him.

The next morning, before Dog had had time to visit the secluded grove, Tortoise went there and sang the song exactly as Dog had sung it. The rope descended to pick him up. But when Tortoise was within a few yards of heaven, Dog's mother looked down and said, "Well, that is not my son," and dropped the rope.

Tortoise fell quickly to earth, badly cracking his shell. He cried for help, attracting some ants who were near that place. They came to him and tried to help him glue his shell together.

As they were working, Tortoise sniffed critically, and said, "Mmm, you ants. Why do you smell so badly?"

The ants were greatly annoyed, and they left him to mend his own condition. That is why the tortoise's shell is cracked and crooked.

 ## Why the Fox Chases the Cock

A long time ago the fox used to run away from the cock because he thought that the cock's comb (crown) was fire. The comb was red, and fire was red. Whenever the rooster appeared, the fox just fled.

The cock was surprised to see the fox run away every time. Finally he managed to get the attention of the fox and he said, "It is so strange that you run away from me. I am just an animal, as you are."

The fox said, "I am afraid of the fire that is on your head."

The cock said, "Why, that is not fire! How could I carry fire on my head and walk around naturally?"

The fox said, "Well, that I do not know."

The cock said, "Touch it. Try it. It is not fire. It will not burn you."

Then, not without fear, the fox touched the comb. And he saw that it was very soft, and not fire at all.

After a while, the fox became accustomed to touching

this comb. And the next thing he thought was, "Well, would this not be a good thing to have for a meal?"

He tried it one time and found that the comb was very delicious. And from that time on, the fox has chased the cock for his comb.

It has been said that the cock has sold himself to the fox, for, if the cock had not been so friendly as to have told the fox that the comb was not fire, he would not have been tormented by the fox.

 ## Why Apes Look Like People

One day the lion, who is taken to be the king of the animals, summoned all the animals to a meeting. The rhinoceros, the elephant, the deer, the fish, the birds, the insects—all assembled, and the lion told them the reason for calling the meeting.

"I have been watching," he began, "and I have seen that human beings are trying to usurp the animals' places. They are not content with their own environment. They have gone into the air by means of airplanes to disturb the birds; they are traveling in the sea, disturbing the fish; they are traveling underground, disturbing the moles and the insects that live in the soil. What shall we do to stop these human beings from usurping our places?"

The animals discussed the matter, but they could not see a solution for the problem. Some suggested that they should wage war against the human beings, but concluded that since they had no machine guns or rifles or other equipment, war would be an unprofitable venture. All of the animals agreed, however, that they must seek a solution.

They turned to the tortoise, who is taken to be the wisest of the animals, and asked his advice. The tortoise said, "Well, the only sensible thing to do is to become men. If all of the animals become human beings, no one will have any advantage over another."

All of the animals agreed that this would indeed solve their problem. But, on the other hand, how could they become human beings? After seeking in vain the answer for this new problem, the animals again consulted the tortoise. "Tell us," they asked, "how we may become human beings."

And the tortoise answered, "I can help you. I will prepare a kettle of medicine, in a very big pot, and each of you shall bathe, one at a time, in the medicine. After your bathing you will become human beings."

All the animals were very happy to learn this, so the tortoise promised to begin preparing the medicine at once. He told them that the medicine would be ready the following day.

These animals went away and got drums and all different kinds of musical instruments. They were very joyful at the prospect of becoming human beings, and they beat drums and danced and sang in their joy. The noise they made was so horrible that it disturbed the tortoise, who was sleeping. He came to see what was happening.

"What is all this noise about?" he asked.

"We are joyful, and we are singing and dancing because by this time tomorrow we shall be human beings."

The tortoise nodded. "Hmmm. So that is your idea! You are still animals; you have not yet become human beings, and you are behaving like this? What more will happen when you have become human beings?" Then the

31

tortoise went away and broke the kettle and let the medicine flow away.

The next day, when the animals got to the spot where they were to bathe and become human beings, they found the broken kettle. Most of the medicine was gone. Some of them were wise enough to scrape up the traces of the medicine and rub it on their bodies. Those few wise ones —and the first to be there—were the apes, the monkeys, the chimpanzees, and the gorillas. These animals therefore resemble human beings more than do other creatures.

 ## Why Twins Are Valued in Serki

A long time ago in a certain area the birth of twins was considered a bad omen for the land. Consequently, twins born in that area were either put to death or thrown into the big forest to be devoured by wild animals. The chief of the village of Serki usually gave the orders for their disposal.

This practice prevailed without exception until certain parents gave birth to especially handsome male twins, light-skinned and well-formed. The twins were so handsome that no eyes could behold them without admiration and at the same time without sorrow that these poor, handsome boys must die. The parents loved their twins so much that they were willing to do anything, even if it should cost them their lives, to preserve the lives of these twins.

As usual, the chief sent for the parents and instructed that the twins be killed. But the parents refused to have their twins destroyed. The chief, in anger, issued an order that the parents with their twins should take their belongings and leave the town immediately, never again to return. The parents agreed, and left.

One of the twins had a black spot on his forehead, and he was called Eiba. The other had two black spots on his forehead, and he was called Saiba. These boys lived with their parents in the forest and grew up to be handsome, strong men. They played together, worked together, and hunted together. They did everything in common.

One day as they were strolling in the forest they saw a man who had been severely wounded and was covered with blood. They were frightened at the sight and were about to take to their heels when the man, in pain, beckoned to them. Being moved with pity, they decided to go and help him.

The man told them that he had been wounded in a battle between his town (Serki, from which the twins and their parents had been driven) and another town. "We are losing fast," he said. "I was forced to leave because I could not fight any more. Please take this amulet," he implored. "Go and help my people if you can." Then he died.

Saiba and Eiba, knowing that Serki was their birthplace, decided to go and help. So they went home and reported the event to their parents, and expressed their wish to go and help the town. The father objected vehemently, saying, "The chief does not want you there and would not even welcome your help. He demanded that your lives be taken, and upon our refusal we were banished from the town." But the two could not be dissuaded. They insisted on going. The mother yielded, and finally the father gave in, too.

So the boys went to fight for the town. Saiba led one battalion and Eiba led another. These young warriors re-

33

deemed all the people and property that had been cap-
tured by the enemy, including the chief's daughter. Two
days later the enemy was forced to flee, thereby making
Saiba and Eiba with their men victorious.

There was a great feasting in celebration of the victory.
At the feast one man announced that there were two
strange faces in their midst. The people then noticed that
the strange faces among them were those of the brave
young soldiers that had led the town to victory. The man,
the twins' uncle, inquired of the chief and the people
whether or not they remembered the faces. Nobody
seemed to remember. The man then reminded them of the
twins—one with a black spot on the forehead and the
other with two spots—that had been banished with their
parents, who had refused to abide by the regulation of
the town to dispose of the twins. "These are the same
twins," he proclaimed.

The chief, remorseful for having driven them away,
asked the twins for forgiveness, which they gave. Then he
sent the two young men back to their parents with many
valuable gifts, as well as soldiers to entreat the parents
to return to the town. The twins and the parents became
the idols of the whole town, the chief included.

From that time on, twins, no longer considered omens
of evil, have been held in high regard.

Moral Fables

 The Tortoise and the
Gourd of Wisdom

The tortoise is considered to be the wisest of all the animals. Well, one day the tortoise decided that he would collect all the wisdom in the earth, put it in a gourd, and hang the gourd on a tree.

At last he had collected, as he thought, all the wisdom in the earth. He packed it into the gourd and tied the gourd around his neck. He began to climb the tree on which he had planned to hang the gourd. But he had great difficulty in climbing the tree since the gourd, hanging around his neck and against his chest, came between him and the tree, causing him to fall. He tried again and again, and fell many times.

There was a man watching him, and finally the man

called to him, "You are supposed to be the wisest animal of all. I will prove to you that you are not wise. Why don't you hang the gourd against your back? Then it will not be in your way when you climb the tree."

The tortoise tried this trick, and he found that he could climb the tree more easily and more quickly—in fact, he could climb the tree. The tortoise was greatly disappointed that he had not truly collected all the world's wisdom in the gourd, that some useful things had been left out. So he broke the gourd, since he could not hope to contain in it all the wisdom in the earth. And that man was considered to be wiser than the tortoise.

Even the wisest of men has moments of foolishness.

 ## The Test

There lived in a city two popular men. One went by the name A-God-Protected-Person-Cannot-Be-Killed-By-King. The other went by the name A-King-Protected-Person-Cannot-Be-Killed-By-God.

There was a king in that city who learned about these men and sent for them. The two came to the king, who asked them their names. They told him. He turned to A-God-Protected-Person-Cannot-Be-Killed-By-King. "Do you really believe in your name?"

"Yes," the man answered the king.

The king then praised him for his boldness and thanked them both for answering to his call. "For your faithfulness and loyalty, have this," the king said, as he gave a white velvet robe to A-God-Protected-Person-Cannot-Be-Killed-By-King and a black velvet robe to A-King-Protected-Person-Cannot-Be-Killed-By-God. But before the king sent the two men away, he instructed a hunter to lie in ambush a few yards from the palace and shoot the man in white velvet.

As they went out, A-King-Protected-Person-Cannot-Be-Killed-By-God looked at his velvet robe and at his partner's. He liked A-God-Protected-Person-Cannot-Be-Killed-By-King's robe better than he did his own. Since A-God-Protected-Person-Cannot-Be-Killed-By-King did not care which robe he had, he readily changed robes with A-King-Protected-Person-Cannot-Be-Killed-By-God. They put their robes on, so that A-God-Protected-Person-Cannot-Be-Killed-By-King was wearing the black velvet robe and A-King-Protected-Person-Cannot-Be-Killed-By-God was wearing the white velvet robe.

As they were going along, there was a loud report and a smoke. A-King-Protected-Person-Cannot-Be-Killed-By-God dropped dead. A-God-Protected-Person-Cannot-Be-Killed-By-King was sore afraid, and ran back and told the king what had happened.

The king was amazed to see A-God-Protected-Person-Cannot-Be-Killed-By-King in a black velvet robe, and to learn how jealous A-King-Protected-Person-Cannot-Be-Killed-By-God had become of the white velvet robe given by the king to A-God-Protected-Person-Cannot-Be-Killed-By-King. The king then confessed what he had ordered done and declared, "There is no king to equal God."

 ## The Man, the Dove, and the Hawk

There was once a man who was both blind and lame. One evening he sat in front of his house and he was very sad about his condition. He could not move and he could not see. He was praying to God.

All of a sudden a dove flew to where he was sitting and hid under his robe. In a second came a hawk, pleading with the man to release the dove to him, for he was very hungry and he had to eat something. If he could not get the dove, he would die. He promised the man that, if he would release the dove to him, he would give the man something to make him see.

The dove pleaded for his life. He told the man that releasing him to the hawk would be releasing him only to his death. If the man would save him, the dove promised, he would give him something to cure his lameness, so that he would be able to walk again.

Then this man was thrown between two stools. He did not know what to do. So he sent for his friend and told him his plight. "Should I gain my sight? Or should I gain my legs?" he asked.

The friend did not know what to tell him. He said at last, "Well, you will have to paddle your own canoe. I cannot help you decide this matter."

The man was very sad because his friend could not help him. He thought for a few minutes. Then he asked the hawk, "Suppose you should get a chicken instead of the dove. Would that be all right?"

The hawk said, "Of course. In fact, I would prefer a chicken to the dove. Because I couldn't get a chicken, I was forced to be content with what I had."

The man said, "Fine." Then he told the dove, "Now, I shall save your life, but you must keep your promise to me." And he said to the hawk, "I shall provide you with food, and you are bound to keep your promise to me."

So the man gave a chicken to the hawk. In return, the hawk told him that he must get a certain leaf, prepare it, and squeeze the juice from it into his eyes. Then he would be able to see again. So the man released the hawk.

After the hawk had gone, he said to the dove, "I have protected you. You must fulfill your promise to me." So the dove told him what he must do to regain the use of his legs. And he released the dove.

The man went according to the instructions of both the birds, the dove and the hawk, and thus he gained not only his sight, but also his legs.

This story teaches us that there are times when we must rely entirely on our own intelligence, rather than try to rely on our friends or other witnesses. If the friend had told him to do one or the other of these things, he would have regained either his sight or his legs, but not both. His friend was a help to him in making him think for himself, thus regaining both his sight and the use of his legs.

 ## The Bellicose Chicken

A hen on training her children instructed them how to fend for themselves. She told them what to do whenever they noticed a hawk around, and especially implored them not to go near or play around any wells in their neighborhood.

One of the young chickens was feeding a few days after that when she noticed a well. Remembering what her mother had told her, she left the vicinity instantly. Another day's feeding brought her near the well again. Instead of leaving, as she had the other day, she stood still, wondering why her mother had instructed her against going near the well. She moved nearer to the well, but nothing happened.

"What on earth can be in this well?" she puzzled. And she became so curious that finally her curiosity overcame her fear. She jumped up on the rim to see what the well contained.

To her surprise, she saw another chicken in the well. She turned her head; the other chicken turned hers, too. She raised her wings; the other chicken did likewise. She chirruped, and the other chirruped, too.

At last, annoyed at this mimicry, she stood her feathers on end and challenged the mimic to a fight. The opponent accepted the challenge by likewise ruffling her feathers. In anger, the young chicken leaped into the well to fight her opponent. But unfortunately there was no chicken to fight except the pool of water. She struggled hard, and cried for help, but nobody was near.

At last she realized that her opponent was her own image. Too late she remembered what her mother had told her, and, regretting her disobedience, she struggled in the well until she weakened and died.

 ## The Lion and the Goat

A goat was one day grazing on a beautiful plain when she was suddenly interrupted by the loud cry of a lion. She looked around and saw the lion in a cage. As she was about to flee from the plain, the lion beckoned to her pleadingly. She drew near the cage.

The lion, starved and fatigued, begged the goat to open

The Lion and the Goat

the cage for him. The goat at first refused, as she did not trust the lion, who might kill her for his meal. On the lion's persistent pleading and his promise to be grateful, the goat opened the cage and the lion walked out.

After the lion was out, he was free to do anything he liked. He thanked the goat for her kindness. The goat had walked a few yards from the cage when the lion changed his mind and decided to kill the goat for his meal, since he was not sure of any other meal and feared dying of starvation. He then ran after the goat and seized her.

The goat was surprised and disappointed to see the lion so ungrateful, and said, "Is it wrong for me to be kind enough to free you from the cage?"

As they were debating the case, a man came to the scene. "What is the trouble?" the man asked. Without wasting a minute the goat stated the case.

"Where is the cage?" the man inquired.

"There." The goat pointed.

"All right, let us go there while you show me how it happened, so I may judge which of you is right." So the lion, the goat, and the man went to the cage.

"Is this the cage you were in?" the man asked the lion.

"Yes."

"In what position were you in the cage?" the man demanded.

"Like this." The lion demonstrated.

The man walked into the cage, sat down, and asked, "Like this?"

"No," the lion said.

"Go in and show me how," the man directed.

The lion walked in. As he was demonstrating the position he had been in, the man quickly locked the cage.

"Yes, that is the reward of ungratefulness," the man

explained. He turned to the goat. "From now on, you will be careful of what you do to help. There is nothing more dangerous than to be kind to a beast."

 ## The Lion, the Tortoise, and the Boar

The big three—the lion, the tortoise, and the boar—representing the members of their groups, decided to establish permanently peaceful living among their groups. But before this goal could be attained, they must themselves be friendly, to impress their followers and set a good example for them. The lion, realizing this situation, advised, "Let us state our dislikes so that we may not offend one another." The others agreed with the lion that his idea was a good one.

The tortoise, the first to state his dislike, explained, "The only thing I abhor is to be spoken of when I am away." The boar, stating his dislike next, said, "I do not mind when or what anybody talks of me, but I do not like anybody to step on my tail." "Neither of these is a problem for me," rejoined the lion, "but I hate to be looked in the face."

They all promised to observe these dislikes and abstain from offending one another. Then the tortoise, excusing himself, left to run an errand. No sooner had he left than the lion remarked, "What does the tortoise think is said of himself when he is away?"

"Perhaps something about his cumbersome shell," remarked the boar.

After a few minutes the tortoise came back. He had hidden among the grasses to hear the remarks made about him when he left. He was unable to think of anything to do about this offense against him. So he gave the lion a nasty look.

The lion, observing this, could think of nothing better to do than fight the tortoise. As they were fighting, the lion stepped on the boar's tail and so the three of them began to fight one another.

The fight was so intense that all the animals came from different directions to watch. Later they too joined in the struggle. Since then, these animals have been sworn enemies.

"To state one's dislike is to initiate one's annoyance" is as true in the animals' world as it is in the humans' world.

 ## The Wasp and the Bee

In the beginning, when God created everything in the earth, he instructed the bee to go into the world. He told him how he could find things and put them together to make a honey that would make everything sweet, and how to build a life that he could enjoy. The bee was very patient. He listened to all the instructions from God. And then he left.

Then came the turn of the wasp. The wasp was very impatient, and he heard only about half of the instructions that God wished to give him. For before God was finished, he took off, saying, "Well, I have everything I need to know."

When he got into the world, the wasp discovered that

he had not received all the instructions. He kept trying to make a honey, but he could not. Instead of making a honey, he made a poison, a venom.

But the bee, who had listened patiently and attentively to God, was able to put together all the things that God had required him to put together, and he could make a honey.

Since then, the bees have been very much liked by the people, whereas the wasp has become the enemy of the people of the earth.

The story teaches us to be patient, and to be attentive to any person who is supposed to instruct us in a certain way.

 ## Three Friends and a Treasure

Three friends were going on a journey and on their way found a bag full of coins. They were very happy, and picked it up.

Soon they came to a stop about a mile away from a town. They were very hungry and decided to buy food to eat. They took just enough money out of the bag to get them a round meal. So the youngest of these men went to the town to buy their food.

After he had left, one of the others suggested that they should kill the youngest so that there would be only two of them to share the treasure. The other, after pondering for a while, refused the proposal. The proposer pressed him to take part in the brutal act, assuring him that no one would know it and telling him a number of things they could do with such a large amount of money. At last the man agreed to the plan, so that they might have more than their share of this treasure they had found.

The youngest man meanwhile got to the town, bought the food, and made for the stopping place. As he was going, a thought flashed through his mind—"If I could kill these two men, all the money would be mine." But there was a voice dinning it in his ears, quietly but persistently, "This would be murder. It would be a blood guilt." These two thoughts kept chasing each other in his head. The noble thought, however, gave way to his greed for the treasure. He returned to the town, bought poison, and put it in the food. "I will tell them that I have taken some fruits in the town and have got no appetite for anything now. They will eat the food and die, and the money will be mine alone," he planned in his mind. After a while, he arrived at the stop with the poisoned food.

Before he returned, the two others had got a good cudgel and a heavy anvil. As he set the food down, without saying anything or allowing him to say anything, they beat him to death. After the brutal act they started eating, but before they could finish the food they dropped dead. The three found the money and died through their own hands and thoughts without sharing a brass farthing out of the huge sum.

 ## The Tortoise and the Hare

The hare always watched the tortoise crawl and made fun of him. One day the hare mockingly challenged the tortoise to a race. The tortoise deliberated on this issue for a while. If he should refuse, the hare's mocking would increase to an intolerable stage. If he should accept, there was no doubt that the hare would win and make him a laughingstock. He could find no way out of the hare's mockery and therefore accepted the challenge.

A day was set for the race and the two were prepared. To the hare it was no problem, but as for the tortoise— that was quite a different matter. They started the race.

After some time, the hare turned back, to see the tortoise a long way behind. He therefore decided to take a nap. The tortoise crawled slowly and resolutely, and overtook and passed the hare silently while the hare slept. The tortoise finally reached the finishing point and shouted, "The slow-but-steady has won the race!"

The hare awoke to see the tortoise ahead of him. He ran fast and galloped violently, but it was too late.

Oh, not to the swift is the race.

 ## The Tortoise and the Boar

The tortoise and the boar were bosom friends and accustomed to dining together. They invited each other to dinner in turns. At last the boar did not want the tortoise to dine with him any more. So when his dinner was ready, he wound himself around the bowl of meal and called the tortoise to dinner.

The tortoise went round and round and finally had stretched to reach the bowl when the boar exclaimed, "Hush! I invited you to dinner and you are stepping on me." The tortoise, after this futile effort to get at the meal, returned to his house, disappointed but resolute.

On the following day, the tortoise prepared his own dinner and tied a rope to his tail which he wound around the bowl of meal. He then hailed the boar for dinner. As the boar stretched to reach the food, the tortoise exclaimed, "Hush! I invited you for dinner and you are stepping on me!"

In amazement, the boar questioned the tortoise, "Since when have you been so big?"

"Man teaches man to be tall or short," answered the tortoise defiantly.

 # The Tortoise and the Snake

At one time the tortoise (*ijapa*) and the snake (*ojola*) were very close friends. They lived together in the same lodge. They ate together out of the same dish. And they were happy.

One day *ojola* was very hungry. "Why should I share this fine food with *ijapa*?" he asked himself. "I shall keep it all to myself." So *ojola* wound his long body around the dish. Nowhere was there a place for *ijapa* to come close enough to the dish to eat.

Ijapa was hungry, too. And in the dish was his favorite porridge, made with yams, with meat and palm oil and condiments. He watched as *ojola* ate. "Why will you not let me at the dish to eat?" asked *ijapa*. "I am hungry, and we have always eaten together."

"I am bigger than you," answered *ojola*. "See. I can wrap myself around the dish. And the food belongs to me

47

because I am big enough to take it for myself." He went on eating. And *ijapa* thought about what *ojola* had said.

The next day *ijapa* made a long tail out of grass. He fastened it to himself. He wound his long tail around the dish of porridge and began to eat. Nowhere was there a place for *ojola* to come close enough to the dish to eat.

Ojola was hungry, too. And in the dish was his favorite porridge, made with yams, with meat and palm oil and condiments. He watched as *ijapa* ate. "Why will you not let me at the dish to eat?" asked *ojola*. "I am hungry. And we have always eaten together."

"Yesterday you were big and I was small," answered *ijapa*. "Today I am big."

So *ojola* watched while *ijapa* finished the porridge.

Need will teach you to be short or to be tall.

 ## The Singing Crow

A hungry fox came out of his hole to see a crow on a tree with a big piece of meat in his beak. "Fine day!" he cried to the crow.

"Hello," mumbled the crow.

"I was just marveling at how wonderful you are," continued the fox. "You have such a beautiful voice that nothing pleases me more than to hear you sing."

"Is that so?" asked the crow, with an air of superiority.

"Of course. I came out purposely to listen to your melodious songs, and I shall be too happy if you will be so kind as to sing one of your lovely songs," entreated the fox.

As the crow opened his beak to sing to impress the fox, his piece of meat fell to the ground. Before he could fly down to recover his meat, the fox had greedily seized it and hurried to his hole.

"Gone is gone—there is no remedy," sighed the crow. "But how foolish was I to have attempted to sing!"

 ## The Country Mouse and the City Mouse

The city mouse was passing by one day and noticed a country mouse eating rotting kernels and discarded peanuts. "Hello, friend," he greeted him.

"Hello," returned the country mouse.

"I am just wondering how you can eat such nasty, stinking food around here," the city mouse continued. "I eat luxurious food any time, and as much as I want. I do not need to labor for my meals," he boasted.

"Is that so?" the country mouse inquired, surprised.

"Surely. Come with me and see. You will love every bit of your time in the city, and never think of coming back."

The country mouse followed the city mouse. At last they entered a big house and found their way into a pantry. There was plenty of food set around. "Come on. Let us eat," the city mouse invited.

No sooner had they started than they heard a sound of footsteps. "Run, run. Run for your life!" the city mouse cried to the country mouse. They both ran out.

The country mouse, with his heart in his mouth, said, "I am going back to the field to eat the nasty food without fear or insecurity, for it is better to be poor and be happy than to be rich and restless."

Envy Can Kill

There was once a man who had two wives. Each of these wives had a daughter. The senior wife was a bad woman —envious and selfish. And the senior wife's daughter, Abeo, was just exactly like her mother—bad and lazy. The second wife was a very good woman—industrious, tolerant, and sympathetic. And her daughter, Alake, danced to her tune. It is so true: like mother, like daughter.

Alake hawked palm oil. She usually left home at dawn and returned at dusk. It happened one day that a man bought palm oil from her, but he had not the right change with him to give to her. The man (who was a ghost in human flesh) asked Alake if she would be willing to follow him to his house to get the change. Alake agreed immediately. The man told Alake the difficulty it would entail before they could get to his place. He told her about the River of Dye and the River of Blood that they would come across on their way. Because Alake was determined, brave, and willing to do any hard work that might bring in some money, the man let her follow him.

They set forth on their journey. They walked and walked and walked until they were near nowhere. Then the man started singing,

"Palm-oil seller, return." [*to be sung by storyteller*]
"*Return? I will not return.*" [*to be sung by audience*]
"Palm-oil seller, return."
"*Return? I will not return.*"
"If you do not return, you will come across the River of Dye."

"Return? I will not return."
"Palm-oil seller, return."
"Return? I will not return."
"Palm-oil seller, return."
"I will not return."

They walked and walked, and after a while they came across the River of Dye. The man started to sing again,

"Palm-oil seller, return."
"Return? I will not return."
"Palm-oil seller, return."
"Return? I will not return."
"If you do not return, you will come across the River of Blood."
"Return? I will not return."
"Palm-oil seller, return."
"Return? I will not return."
"Palm-oil seller, return."
"I will not return."

After they had walked for some time, they came to the River of Blood.

Shortly after that, they arrived at the man's house. The man praised Alake for her perseverance and gave her the money for the palm oil. In addition, he told her to go to his back yard, where she would find many gourd trees. "Some of the gourds will be very attractive and some will be dull and unattractive. But you should pick three dull gourds," the man instructed her. "Break one of the gourds at the junction of the four roads," the man continued, "the second in your own back yard, and the third one behind the closed door of your mother's room." Alake followed the man's instructions diligently.

When she broke the first one, there appeared servants and attendants that followed her. Then she broke the second one, and what did she find? Boxes of expensive and fine clothes, and many kinds of wealth. The servants and attendants carried these goods for her and followed her. When she got home her parents were surprised to see her with so many servants, all carrying goods. They welcomed her warmly. Shortly after her arrival, she went into her mother's room with her mother, locked the door, and broke the third and last gourd. What appeared? Gold and silver jewelry, precious beads, and rare stones of all kinds. These made Alake and her mother rich.

Since Alake and her mother were very kind and generous, they divided their wealth into three parts. They gave one part to Alake's father and another to the senior wife, and kept the third part themselves. But the senior wife, because of her envy, refused to take anything from them. She insisted on knowing how they had come by their wealth, so she could do the same thing.

In no time at all, the senior wife had made a palm-oil seller out of her lazy daughter, Abeo. She left home at dawn and returned at dusk. And one day a man bought palm oil from her, but he had not the right change with him to give to her. The man asked Abeo if she would be willing to follow him to his house to get the change. Abeo agreed immediately. The man told Abeo the difficulty it would entail before they could get to his place. He told her about the River of Dye and the River of Blood that they would come across on their way. Because Abeo was eager to obtain for herself riches even greater than those that had fallen to Alake, she insisted upon following the man.

They set forth on their journey. They walked and walked and walked until they were near nowhere. Then the man started singing,

"Palm-oil seller, return." [*storyteller*]
"Return? I will not return." [*audience*]
"Palm-oil seller, return."
"Return? I will not return."
"If you do not return, you will come across the River of Dye."
"Return? I will not return."
"Palm-oil seller, return."
"Return? I will not return."
"Palm-oil seller, return."
"I will not return."

They walked and walked, and after a while they came across the River of Dye. The man started to sing again,

"Palm-oil seller, return."
"Return? I will not return."
"Palm-oil seller, return."
"Return? I will not return."
"If you do not return, you will come across the River of Blood."
"Return? I will not return."
"Palm-oil seller, return."
"Return? I will not return."
"Palm-oil seller, return."
"I will not return."

After they had walked for some time, they came to the River of Blood.

Shortly after that, they arrived at the man's house. The man praised Abeo for her perseverance and gave her the money for the palm oil. In addition, he told her to go to his back yard, where she would find many gourd trees. "Some of the gourds will be very attractive and some will be dull and unattractive. But you should pick three dull gourds," the man instructed her. "Break one of the gourds at the junction of the four roads," the man continued,

53

"the second in your own back yard, and the third one behind the closed door of your mother's room." But Abeo, instead of following the man's instructions, picked the three most attractive gourds she could find.

When she broke the first gourd, many poisonous insects appeared and started to sting her. She took to her heels. She broke the second gourd when she came to her own back yard and there appeared huge gorillas and wild monkeys who started to beat her. She still had not given up the hope of wealth, so she entered her mother's room with her mother, locked the door, and broke the third gourd. What happened? All kinds of poisonous snakes and dangerous animals imaginable appeared and devoured them.

This story teaches us that the envious invite trouble upon their heads.

Trickster

Tales

 Just Say "Ree"

A lawyer, learning that his neighbor was involved in a theft case, went to him. "If you will share the money with me, I will set you free," he offered.

"Can you, really?" the criminal inquired, doubting that this thing could be done.

"Yes. Why not?" the lawyer answered, full of confidence.

"All right. I shall give you half of the money if you can," the thief agreed.

The criminal's employer had sued him, and the date of the hearing was at hand. "What you have to do is to pretend madness," the lawyer explained. "To any question whatsoever asked of you, just say 'Ree,' " the lawyer directed.

"Oh, my. That's simple," the criminal observed. He agreed to do as he was counseled.

The day came and the case was called in the court. "Mr. Bobo, it was reported that on so-and-so date such-and-such amount of money was missing in the section where you were working. What do you know about it?" the Crown Counsel asked firmly.

"Ree," the criminal answered.

The Crown Counsel repeated his statement and Bobo said repeatedly, "Ree, ree."

"You are Mr. Bobo?" the judge inquired.

"Ree, ree" was the only answer to that question and every succeeding one. The lawyer stood up and asked for dismissal of the case, as his client had been suffering from a mental derangement for the past few weeks and he was quite sure that some scamps had taken advantage of his mental depression to get away with the money in question. After much argument between the lawyer and the Crown Counsel, the case was dismissed by the judge.

When the court was over, the lawyer took his client home to get his own share of the money. "The case is now over and you are free. What about my own share?" the lawyer demanded as they sat together in the living room.

"Ree," was the client's answer.

"Be serious now and make haste."

"Ree" was still the only audible sound.

"I am serious. I have an appointment at five o'clock. Be sober and give me my share."

Every effort to make his client sane after the temporary madness proved useless. The lawyer, disappointed and chagrined, went away angry with himself that he had not taken his share before the trial.

The Three Tasks

A man in a fairly well populated town had a beautiful daughter. So beautiful was she that not only the nobles of the town proposed to marry her, but also kings and princes from surrounding towns. Her father defeated these suitors by setting three tasks, none of which any of them could perform. A clever farmer about fifty miles from the town heard about the matter and decided to go for a trial.

The first of the tasks was to stay in a room full of mosquitoes without moving or driving the mosquitoes away when thousands of them alighted on the suitor's naked body and bit him. The second task was to eat a well-ground red-hot pepper without showing any sign of pain or any twisting of the lips to ease the painful action of the pepper. And the third task was to tell a story that would last for a whole day—from dawn to dusk.

At the first task, the farmer pretended to describe to his watchful guards a peculiar horse that he had seen on his way. He slapped his body at different places to indicate the colorful spots on the white horse as he said, "There was white here, black there, yellow at this spot, green at that, and white everywhere." In this way he discreetly drove the mosquitoes away, while the guards took him seriously and expressed their amazement. The period for staying in the room elapsed. The guards had not seen him drive away the mosquitoes—deliberately but cunningly— and they proclaimed him a successful performer of the first task.

The second task was to eat hot pepper without squinting or grimacing or using any gesture to suggest the biting action of the pepper on the tongue. The farmer before he sat down to his fateful meal threw some corn on the ground near the spot where he was to sit, to attract the chickens in the yard. As these fowls drew near him in an attempt to pick up the corn, he complained, "These fowls are pestering me. Zoo, zoo, zoo!" He drove them away, waving his hands. So he cunningly ate up the pepper without apparent gesture to show or ease the pain of the hot pepper on his tongue.

The last task was to tell a story continuously from morning till night. The day dawned only too quickly, and the farmer determined to attack this last task with courage, to win the most cherished beauty of the town.

"During the last harvest," the farmer began, "I packed many bags of corn in my barn. Soon I detected the presence of a mouse in and around the barn. To be sure whether my idea was correct or not, I decided to watch. Within an hour I saw a mouse gnawing at a bag until a hole resulted. Then he picked up one grain, ran to his nest, came back, picked up another and ran to his nest. I stood motionless and he picked up another and picked up another and picked up another and picked up another . . ." the farmer repeated, until everyone in the audience had become bored and darkness covered the sky.

The father, unable to gainsay or disqualify the farmer, had no choice other than to give his daughter in marriage to the only successful suitor.

The Tortoise and
the Tug of War

Everybody knows that the hippopotamus is very strong. In fact, he is considered one of the strongest of all the animals.

Well, one day the tortoise went to the hippopotamus and he said to him, "You are thought to be so strong. But would you be surprised if I told you that I could pull you out of the river?"

The hippopotamus smiled at the tortoise. "What! You are joking! Pull me out of the river? You are too small. It cannot be done."

"But I can do it," the tortoise insisted.

"I would be very much surprised if you did," said the hippopotamus. "But I am willing to try it."

So the tortoise set a date with the hippopotamus to try their strength.

Then the tortoise went to the elephant. "You are so strong," he said. "But can you believe that I can pull you into the river?"

"Impossible!" said the elephant. "You are too small."

"But I am sure I can do it," insisted the tortoise.

"Well, then, we will try," agreed the elephant. And a date was set for the trial—the same date that had been set with the hippopotamus.

The tortoise got a very strong rope. And on the day set for the trial, everybody was there, to see what would happen.

The tortoise went down into the river and gave one end of the rope to the hippopotamus. "Hold this," he said.

59

"But do not begin pulling until I tug on the rope. Then you can start."

The tortoise went up out of the water as if he were ready to pull against the hippopotamus. But he went up to the elephant. He gave him the other end of the rope. "Hold this," he said. "But do not begin pulling until I tug on the rope. Then you can start."

Then he left the elephant and made as if he were going into the water to pull against him. But he went just to the edge of the water and tugged at the rope. Then he hid.

The hippopotamus and the elephant began to pull. They tried their best to pull each other either way. And this tug of war went on from morning till afternoon.

Finally the hippopotamus thought, with surprise, "Can it be true that the tortoise is this strong?" And at the same time, the elephant thought to himself, "Can it be possible that the tortoise is this strong?"

The hippopotamus became so curious that his curiosity overshadowed his reluctance to being defeated by the tortoise. And he began walking slowly up out of the deep part of the river toward the land, to see whether indeed it was the tortoise pulling on the other end of the rope.

And the elephant became so curious that his curiosity finally overshadowed whatever honor he might achieve at winning the contest. And he began walking slowly toward the river's edge to see whether it was truly the tortoise who was pulling on the other end of the rope.

When the elephant and the hippopotamus met in the shallow water at the edge of the river, they found that they had been pulling against each other. But the elephant *had* been pulled into the river, and the hippopotamus *had* been pulled out of the river, by the clever tortoise.

Strength may lie in wit, as well as in muscle.

The Elephant and the Tortoise

The king of a certain town became ill, and the native doctors had to be called in. On examining the king, the doctors said that it would be necessary to get the heart of an elephant to cure the king.

Now this is not something easily come by. So the king's bellman was sent out to try to get someone who would agree to provide the elephant's heart. Nobody was willing to do so, because it entailed so much risk.

Finally the tortoise came forward and promised that within seven days he would provide the native doctors with the heart of an elephant. He asked for certain things. One of them was one of the cloths [robes] usually worn by the king. The second was the usual food eaten by the king. With these materials the tortoise went into the forest.

He looked around for some time and at last he was able to contact an elephant. When he got to the elephant, he prostrated himself before the elephant, which is the usual way of greeting a king-elect. The elephant did not understand what the tortoise was trying to do. The tortoise told him that the king had died, and that the king makers had decided on making an elephant the king. The elephant couldn't believe his ears. This was too strange to be true.

The tortoise did not get up; he remained in that crouched position. He gave the elephant a piece of the food which he had, saying that that was what he had been asked by the king makers to give to the new king. "This is just a taste of what the king usually has," the tortoise declared. Now, the elephant just couldn't believe it.

Well, he went further, and he gave the elephant the cloth he had brought along. Then he said the elephant should start back with him at once, so that he would get to the town in good time for his coronation.

The elephant had a friend, a small bird. The small bird had been in town while the king's bellman had been going around trying to find someone willing to provide the heart of an elephant. So the small bird told the elephant that the tortoise had come to play a trick on him. But the elephant refused to believe this.

The small bird kept telling the elephant not to go. He started to sing a little song, and in it warned the elephant not to trust this new friend but to stay where he could depend on his old friends. The elephant listened and began to doubt the tortoise.

The tortoise feared that he was going to be defeated in his purpose, so he began to sing another song, telling all about the honors that would fall to the elephant when he became king. The elephant listened to the tortoise, and he began to fancy himself as king.

At this, his old friend began to worry about the effect the tortoise's song was having on the elephant, and he began to sing his warning song again. The tortoise broke in on the bird's song with his own tempting offer of kingship and the honors that went with it. And every time he thought the elephant was becoming suspicious, he would give the elephant part of the food he had brought along. When the elephant would eat, the food tasted good, so he went along slowly with the tortoise toward the town. As they went along, the little bird continued to sing his warning song, but the elephant no longer heeded it.

At last they came to the town. The king makers had

arranged to have the whole place lined with people. All these people were cheering the elephant, the king-elect. The tortoise was prostrating himself before the elephant. The people were shouting, "Here comes our new king."

The king makers had arranged a raised platform, and right under this platform a deep hole had been dug. When the elephant arrived on the platform his weight caused the platform to give way and he fell down into the hole. He was unable to climb out again. And people beat the elephant until he died. Thus the tortoise provided the native doctors with the heart of an elephant.

This story has a moral, as all Yoruba stories have: One should rely more on his old friends than on new ones, and whenever possible he should use his own judgment. If it had been decided to make the elephant king, someone of greater consequence than the tortoise would have been sent. The elephant ought to have known that.

 ## The Girl Who Knew the King

There was once a certain king whose breakfast always consisted of *akara* [fried cake made of bean flour] and *ako* [a custardlike food made from corn meal]. The *akara* was always supplied by the same girl. This girl, every time she went to the palace of the king, would stop by to see the king's parrot. She would give the parrot a piece of *akara* while she waited to serve the *akara* to the king.

Then, to one girl after another, she began to boast that she knew the king. This was a serious thing to do.

The king is believed to be God's anointed, God's representative on earth. It is a wild claim to make, to say that a woman, of all people, knows the king. This girl, being young and thoughtless, went about telling people that she knew the king and could identify him anywhere.

Now this came to the ears of the king, and it was arranged that she could come out and identify the king. On the day of the test, the king was not dressed in his usual fashion. He wore tattered clothes. His hair was uncombed, and his nails were uncut. He was barefooted. Even one very close to the king would have found great difficulty in recognizing him. Then the girl was brought into the palace, in front of all the people, and told to identify the king.

Very fortunately for her, the parrot had escaped from his cage, and he came to her aid. He started to sing. Now, what the parrot was saying was, "There is the king, dressed in rags. There is the king. Just watch the way I point my feathers. There is the king there, dressed in tattered clothes. There is the king!" And the parrot pointed his wings toward the king.

The king's friends became annoyed at the noise of the parrot, and they tried to catch him. But the parrot flew up out of their reach and began to sing again, the same song. He repeated that she should follow the direction of his feathers to find the king.

Every time the parrot sang, the members of the court became more angry, until at last they resolved to kill him. But he flew a short distance away and came back again. He sang many times, until the girl knew what the parrot was singing and could identify the king.

Since she had been able to identify the king, the king had to give her half of his worldly belongings, and the girl and her family became wealthy.

The Body in the Coffin

One time in a small town, meat was so scarce that it could not be had for love or money. In the course of time, two young men discovered that hogs were being raised in a nearby town. They begged the owner to sell some —or one, at least. But he refused to sell, so they were compelled to resort to other means of getting a hog, since they needed meat badly. The only means that was open was stealing.

But how could they get the hog to their town without detection? That posed a nice problem. After giving the problem much thought, they arrived at a clever means of transporting the hog to their town.

Secretly and carefully they went before dawn one day to the place where the hogs were kept. They got hold of one of the hogs, killed it, and put it into a coffin that they had taken along with them. By sunup they were on their way back to their own town, carrying the coffin and singing songs of mourning.

Two travelers coming toward these corpse-bearers were arguing between themselves in this fashion:

"The man in the coffin might not be completely dead," said one of them.

"I am sure the body is entirely lifeless," the other asserted firmly.

"How can you be so sure?" questioned the first traveler.

"If you doubt my assurance, let us ask the bearers," the second man suggested.

"Yes, by all means," agreed the first.

The question posed by these two travelers puzzled the coffin-bearers, and they could not but misinterpret the question. Panic seized them. Their consciences smote them. Aggressive attack appeared the only answer for this challenging question.

The fiasco resulted in a summons for all four of them to appear before the local chief. After much questioning, the chief demanded an examination of the coffin. The coffin was examined and found to contain neither a half-dead person nor a corpse, but a big, fresh hog.

The two young men were accused of stealing. Though they pleaded for leniency and explained the necessity that had driven them to stealing the hog, they found themselves subject to three years' confinement as a punishment for their bold act.

 ## The Right Recompense

The tortoise, meeting the lion one day, remarked, "The animals in this area are becoming swollen-headed. They move about carelessly, with no regard for their own safety."

"Oh?" queried the lion, surprised. "I have been looking for animals lately and have found not a one."

The tortoise, who knew the lion's need for animal flesh for food and his desire to get any of these careless walkers, promised to show him where the animals were if he would follow and obey him. The lion agreed, and followed the tortoise, confident of a fine dinner.

Before the tortoise had left home, he had instructed his wife to prepare a barrel of boiling water. When the

lion and the tortoise were within a stone's throw of the
tortoise's house, the tortoise persuaded the lion to crawl
into a big bag which he was carrying. "In this way, the
animals will not recognize you," he said.

The starved and docile lion agreed. "That is a good
idea. They might otherwise run away and escape," he
remarked, as he walked freely and happily into the bag.

The tortoise with all his power tied up the bag very
tightly and carried it to his own home on his back. As he
approached his wife and children, they welcomed him and
asked how he had been. The tortoise, under a heavy
strain, did not answer, but beckoned for them to be quiet
and to take the cover off the barrel of boiling water. The
tortoise, shuffling one foot after the other but with a determined effort, staggered to the barrel and dumped the
lion, bag and all, into the boiling water.

There was a great struggling and splashing in the barrel for a while, followed by occasional whirling and ter-
minated by perfect stillness. And this was how the animal
terrorist traced his dinner to the grave.

 ## The Lovers

There lived a couple in a small but famous town. The
two had been happy for some time after their marriage.
But as time went on, the wife became dissatisfied with her
husband for certain reasons. She could no longer find the
happiness she wanted in her home and therefore resorted
to making secret love with young men in the neighborhood. The husband's friends told him about his wife's
unfaithfulness, but he paid no heed to it.

The husband of the unfaithful wife worked in the

evenings, which served as favorable times for the visits of the secret lovers. One day the husband was sick and returned home earlier than usual. The secret lovers did not know that the husband was at home. As usual, one of them strolled into the back yard with the hope of going in to chat with the woman. He was about to enter when the woman signaled to him that her husband was in. Confused and embarrassed, he leaped into the big pot standing in the back yard, to hide.

Some time after that came another of the lovers. It was getting dark, and the woman was unable to signal the man before he entered. The man shivered and trembled as he found himself before the husband.

"Whom are you looking for?" the husband demanded indignantly.

The unfortunate man, at his wits' end, said, "I want to carry to my farm the big pot that is in the back yard, and I am looking for somebody to help me lift it up onto my back."

"Oh, I can help you," the husband said readily, as he rose and followed the man to the pot.

"The pot is quite heavy," the lover commented as the husband of the woman was lifting the pot with him.

After leaving the husband with his wife and walking for a few yards with a heavy pot on his back, the man began to berate himself. "What trouble I have created for myself," he grumbled.

"Hnh. Your situation is better than mine, in this terribly hot pot," commented the man in the pot.

"What!" the man exclaimed, frightened almost to death. And he dropped the pot and ran away.

Fertility Tales

 The Promise

One of the wives of a certain farmer was barren. And this is a very unfortunate thing for a woman in a Yoruba community. Any woman who is without child is always the object of ridicule among the other wives of the husband.

Now this woman was very unfortunate. She had no children at all, and she was advanced in age. Continually the other wives would poke fun at her, until at last she decided that she would go to the god in the forest and talk to him about having children. That is the practice in that part of Nigeria; a woman who is childless goes to the god in the forest and makes some promises in return for a child.

FERTILITY TALES

This woman, because she had no child and had become advanced in age, made a very wild promise. The other women who went to the god promised and brought goats and sheep. This woman, instead of promising goats and sheep, which she could afford, promised she would give the god her first-born child. This was an extravagant promise to make, but since she had made it she was bound to keep it.

The god then gave her some medicine. She went back, and after a while she started to have children. Now the other women went back to the god and paid the god for what he had done. Whatever they had promised to pay, they paid. But this woman did not. She couldn't go to the god because it seemed too serious a thing to have to give a child away. And the first-born was light-skinned, and very beautiful.

After a while the god went to her and demanded that she live up to her promise. She started to tremble; she started to cry. She sang a mournful, pleading song, but the god was not moved. So she went to her husband and told him the promise she had made. There was nothing anybody could do. She had to give her first-born child away. And that was how this woman lost her first child.

This story has a moral, too, and this is it: a man should not make a promise which he feels he cannot live up to. It is not necessary to promise to give something very big. If a man cannot give something, it is not sensible to promise to give it. A small gift is better than a promise to give something large that you cannot realize.

Three Wives and a Porridge

Once a man married three wives, and none of them gave birth to a child. Worried because none of his wives had borne a child, the man went to a diviner to consult with him about what might be done to enable his wives to bear children.

The diviner prepared a certain porridge to be taken by the wives, and he told the man that if this medicine was taken by the wives they would surely conceive. The medicine to produce fertility was already in the porridge.

The man carried the porridge home and explained to his three wives what the diviner had told him—that the porridge contained a medicine which would enable them to conceive and bear children. Each of the wives was to eat of this porridge.

Now two of the wives, bearing ill feelings toward the third wife, contrived to send her out on an errand. In her absence, they ate up all of the porridge. When she returned, she found all of the porridge finished except for a small remnant which clung to the bottom of the pot. There was nothing for her to do but to peel out the remnant and eat it.

Fortunately for this woman, the medicine in the porridge had settled to the bottom, and what she scraped up and ate was the part which would produce fertility. She therefore conceived. And what the other two wives had eaten was merely porridge, so they were unable to conceive. They were not very happy about this.

As the other wives realized that the third wife would

deliver a child, they planned another trick, to deprive her of her child. At the time she was about to give birth, the jealous wives got a stone of about the size of a newborn baby, and they splashed it with blood. While they were helping this wife in childbirth, one of them removed her baby and slipped under her the blood-smeared stone.

As soon as the wife was conscious after giving birth to her baby, she requested to see the baby. The other wives presented her with the blood-smeared stone, saying that that was what had been inside her—that was her baby.

The wife was very sad about this, and she could not believe it. Meanwhile, the other wives had taken the baby to some other people in a nearby town who would care for it.

One day this third wife happened to go to the market place and she heard the news about her child. She saw the child and recognized certain resemblances between herself and the child. So she went to her husband and told him what had happened.

It was arranged that the ownership of the child would be put to a test. Each of the three wives was told to prepare a certain kind of food to set before the child. The child would be invited to attend the ceremony, and to taste of any dish which he desired. The dish from which he chose to eat, it was believed, would be the one prepared by his rightful mother.

The child's mother, who was not liked by the other two wives and was quite poor, was unable to secure fine foods, and the dish which she prepared was not appetizing. The other two wives pooled their resources and prepared delicious and good-looking foods certain to attract the child. The child was then called to taste the dishes.

No one thought that the child would be attracted by the food his own mother had prepared, since it was the least appetizing. But to the surprise of the two jealous wives, the child went straight to the unappetizing dish prepared by his mother, and ate of it. That woman was therefore declared to be the mother of the child, and her child was returned to her.

The Man and the Fertility Porridge

A man was greatly troubled about the sterility of his wife, and he went to a diviner to get his help. The diviner prepared him a porridge, but before giving it to him the diviner warned him not to eat any of it. Even if a bit of the porridge should spill on his hand, he should try to wash it off. He should not lick it, or let a bit of the porridge touch his tongue. The man agreed that he would not eat of the porridge.

On the way to his home there was a stone, and accidentally the man stumbled, and the pot containing the porridge broke. The soup spilled over. He saw that the porridge was very interesting and good-looking, and he was greatly tempted to lick his finger. He decided that would be a very foolish thing to do. But the more he decided not to do it, the more attractive and appetizing this porridge became.

At last he could no longer avoid the temptation, and he licked his finger. He gathered up what remained in the broken pot to take home to his wife. But before he got home, the porridge tempted him so greatly that he ate up almost half of what remained.

So it happened that not only the wife conceived, but he, too, conceived. And this was very ridiculous and unusual, for it was unheard-of for a man to conceive a child.

As it came near the time for the man and his wife to bear the children they had conceived, the man became worried. It was clearly impossible for him to deliver a child. So he went back to the diviner who had given him the medicine, to get ' is help.

The diviner said he was very sorry, but that he had warned the man not to allow any of the medicine to touch his tongue and the man had not heeded his warning. There was nothing that he could do to help. The man had made his bed and therefore he must lie on it.

 ## The Tortoise and the Forbidden Porridge

The tortoise became so worried about the barrenness of his wife that he decided to consult the diviner, that he might obtain a cure. The diviner promised to help him. With considerable care and effort, the diviner prepared a medicinal porridge and handed it to the tortoise in a closed calabash.

"This is an infallible cure for barrenness," the diviner declared. "Do not open it. Just give it to your wife and tell her to take all of it."

The tortoise grabbed the calabash and went happily homeward. As he was going along, an appetizing smell assailed his nostrils. "Such a delicious smell could surely not come from this medicine," he said to himself. He sniffed and sniffed, and, unable to detect the source of the appetizing odor, the tortoise laid the calabash on the ground and went to seek out the good-smelling food. To his surprise, he realized that the farther he walked from the porridge calabash, the less intense the pleasant odor became. He finally discovered that the odor came from the porridge he was bearing to his wife.

So appetizing was the odor that came from the forbidden magical soup that the tortoise could not resist the temptation of going against the diviner's instructions. After much deliberation, he yielded to temptation, contenting himself by believing that opening the calabash to see what was inside could do him no harm. On seeing the porridge, the tortoise felt a greater temptation to taste it than he had had to open the calabash. His saliva was flowing; his tongue was twisting; he felt very, very hungry. Without allowing himself further deliberation, he tasted the porridge.

In rapid order, he went from tasting to drinking, and from drinking to draining. Before he realized fully his unscrupulous behavior and the consequence it might bring, his belly had swollen to an unbelievable size. The tortoise became much afraid. Despondent and perplexed, he returned to the diviner to plead guilty and to beseech him to cure him of his pregnancy.

"Irrevocable is my decision, and my instruction is absolute," sternly declared the diviner.

"My disobedience was not intentional," pleaded the tortoise. "I tumbled over a stump and the soup splashed all over my body and accidentally got into my mouth." But this explanation was unsuccessful in winning the diviner's mercy.

In this hopeless situation the tortoise returned home. Unable to confess his misadventure to his wife, he suffered silently and finally died of the pregnancy which he had sought for his wife. And well he knew before he died that pregnancy can be dangerous.

Notes

 ## Tales of Demon Lovers

These tales belong with a large area of folklore having to do with otherworldly lovers or, as they are frequently called, demon lovers. Sometimes the nonmortal mates come from the realm of the gods, as in the Cupid and Psyche story; sometimes they are fairy lovers, like the Queen of Elfland met on the mead by Thomas Rhymer of the old Scottish ballad. Sometimes they are nymphs, centaurs, satyrs, mermen, mermaids. Often they are associated in some way with the animal kingdom. They may be wild beasts miraculously transformed into human shape, or, quite the reverse, they may, following the Beauty-and-the-Beast pattern, be mortals enchanted for a prescribed period of time to appear in animal shape. Most of the material in this section would seem to be of rather ancient origin.

The Hunter and the Deer

This is a variant of what is probably the most widely distributed tale about otherworldly lovers, the Swan Maiden story. In its essential features the Swan Maiden story is a simple one. A young man comes upon a group of girls swimming in a lake. While observing them, he notices on the shore, instead of ordinary clothing, several sets of

77

swan feathers, and he realizes then that the girls are really creatures of the nonhuman world. By hiding one set of feathers he makes it impossible for the owner to return to her swan form, and thus he wins a beautiful wife. Usually, however, the maiden, either by accident or through the design of an enemy, later finds her swan clothes again, and, impulsively donning them, returns once more to her original form.

In Olawale Idewu's tale, a deer (or antelope) is substituted for the swan, and the hero is a hunter—adaptations necessary to root the action unmistakably in Yoruba culture. And here, as in "The Hunter Who Was King," which follows in this section, the strong didactic emphasis of Nigerian folk tales is evident: one does not always get a second chance in this life. Ordinarily in tales of this type, the mortal mate who violates some tabu in his relationship with an otherworldly lover is given an opportunity to redeem his error. Thus Psyche does not lose Cupid forever, nor does the tale "East of the Sun and West of the Moon" end in tragedy when the heroine steals the forbidden look at her bear-prince. In fact, the Swan Maiden frequently has as a sequel another tale, such as The Man on a Quest for His Lost Wife (Type 400) or The Search for the Lost Husband (Type 425). In "The Hunter and the Deer" oathbreaking is fatal.

Allowing for such deviations, however, the story is one that follows rather closely what seems to be a pattern archetypal in the folk imagination, a pattern used by widely separated peoples between whom no communication is known to exist. Two tabus common in this type are violated here: 1) the spouse is forbidden to reveal to anyone the true nature of the demon lover; and 2) the transformed person is not to have her original nature mentioned to her face thereafter. This latter tabu is especially strong in some North American Indian tribes, where fox-women and bison-women are known to return immediately to their animal kin if their origins are indiscreetly mentioned. So inviolable are these tabus that listeners in an oral culture undoubtedly sense impending tragedy as soon as one is broken. For an interesting African treatment of the latter tabu, see Melville Herskovits, ed., "Bulu Tales from the Collection of A. N. Krug," *JAF*, LXII (1949), 358–359.

As was noted in the Introduction, there are several distortions, apparently conscious ones, which occur in this version of the traditional tale. These were doubtless made in order to fit the story to a Western listener, and for the most part they tend to modernize the setting. The use of the word "attic" is a good example. Perhaps the most notable modernization, however, occurs in the nature of the moral. Ordinarily, there would be no objection in Nigerian society to multiple wives. The Christian orientation of Mr. Idewu's missionary schooling and mature years may account for this paradox.

Except where otherwise indicated, this and all succeeding tales were told to us by Olawale Idewu.

The Hunter and the Witch

The eagerness of the hunter to win the woman in this tale is in part motivated by her beauty and in part by an economic consideration. Here a seemingly desirable wife can be his without the payment of a bride price.

The demon lover of this tale is a figure more sinister than the Swan Maiden. Although at first glance she does not seem to be an ordinary witch, she does retain several of the qualities attributed to witches over the ages. She is, for example, a protean creature, changing shape as the occasion demands. To turn into a mass of teeth is not a common transformation, even for a witch, in Western tales; but to appear to the hero as a beautiful woman is a favorite stratagem (Motif G264). Her desire for human blood (Motif G262.1) suggests the behavior of a vampire, but it should be remembered that she differs from these ghoulish beings in that she is a live woman and not one of the walking dead. It is more likely that there is an influence here of wer-creatures, especially the wer-hyena, a familiar figure in African folk tales.

The finality of a third attempt—three times and out—is one of the commonest of folk beliefs; the witch-wife's fourth attempt was in the folk tradition foredoomed to failure. The tree-to-tree escape, the creature who fells successive trees with its teeth, and the final rescue by faithful dogs are elements found in several African tales outside Nigeria. See, for example, the story of Kchodo-moduno in C. Hoffman, "Märchen und Erzählungen der Eingeborenen in Nord-Transvaal," *Zeitschrift für Kolonialsprachen,* VI (1915), No. 46, 305ff.

The Hunter Who Was King

Among the folk tales of the world there are more than sixty recorded motifs for Unique Prohibitions and Compulsions. Perhaps the most familiar is that of the Forbidden Chamber (C611), used in the story of Bluebeard, who concealed the bodies of his murdered wives in that special room. For an African variant of this story transported to America, see Elsie Clews Parsons, *Folk-Lore*

of the Sea Islands, South Carolina, p. 47; for a similar
version told among white Americans in the South, see
Ralph Boggs, "North Carolina White Folktales and Riddles," *JAF,* XLVII (1934), 295.

"The Hunter Who Was King" turns upon a closely
related motif, The Forbidden Door (C611.1); as is
often the case with this motif, there is no obvious point to
the prohibition. There is nothing concealed by the door;
there is simply a tabu against opening it. At times such
a tabu provides a means of testing the hero's or heroine's
obedience or fidelity: he or she has *agreed* to forgo looking into the room. The punishment for disobedience,
usually harsh, may be death or, as here, paradise irrev-
ocably lost. The hunter of this tale realizes the heights
of prestige and comfort, but then, falling prey to his
curiosity, he loses all. As in "The Hunter and the Deer,"
there is no second chance. There operates concurrently a
further testing of the hunter's integrity—one to which a
Nigerian audience would be alert—in the temptation to
ignore the diviner's command to be satisfied with whatever he found. Content at first to pursue the seemingly
worthless alligator, the hunter at last succumbs to the
dissatisfaction against which he had been cautioned.

Time often has a special dimension in tales of enchantment. The years that the hunter spends in the other-
world of this tale—he is there long enough to see numerous progeny growing up—are as but a day in the
sight of the sun. When he is eventually disenchanted, it
is still the same day, for only a few hours of human
time have elapsed. He picks up his hunting equipment—
anachronistically a gun and a cutlass—at the spot where
he dug for the alligator and, going home, finds the same
world that he left. Sometimes, as in the Rip Van Winkle
type, time is telescoped in the other direction.

The Wolf-Prince

This could well be considered a trickster tale: a perceptive young man exploits a rash father by means of a disguise and thereby wins his beautiful daughter. But there is also here a similarity to a very large group of tales that tell of enchanted husbands or lovers who are finally disenchanted (Type 425). It is like the fairy tale of Beauty and the Beast, long a favorite of young readers and moviegoers.

In all of these tales a girl is committed to marriage with a monster—sometimes because of a debt that the father cannot pay in any other coin, and sometimes because the girl inadvertently incurs the wrath of a witch or some other evil spirit. As it often turns out, the monster she weds was a human being to begin with—sometimes he is a long-lost fiancé—but was enchanted to appear as a repulsive or ferocious beast. He can escape the spell only when a beautiful woman comes to love him in all his hideousness. This the wife finally does, and at that point he changes into a handsome prince and the story ends happily. As we hear this Nigerian tale, we, the listeners, know all along that the wolf is simply a disguised lover, but parallels to the basic Beauty-Beast type remain: the father, in a moment of rashness, involves himself in a dangerous and inescapable commitment; he pays the price of his impulsiveness with the loss of his beloved daughter; the daughter, dutiful at the crucial point, obeys her father's orders and marries the wolf; the beast becomes the stock fairy-tale prince, and tragedy is transformed to romance.

Pourquoi Stories

Every primitive culture has tales to explain how things in nature came to be the way they are. Like the Moral Fables of the next section, these etiological tales seem to us to be intended primarily for children, but they probably come closer to what most authorities would agree are myths. The *pourquoi*—also known as the *why* story or the *just-so* story—does, of course, have a perennial appeal to children. Cub Scouts delight in such American Indian *pourquois* as "How the Loon Got His Necklace," and readers over the years have enjoyed Kipling's literary adaptation of the type in his juvenile *Just-So Stories*.

Universal as the type is, the details vary sharply from one place to another, and there are probably fewer *close* analogues in other cultures for these stories than there are for any other grouping in this volume. One *pourquoi*, "Why Apes Look Like People," does show the influence of non-African culture. Here is an ancient tale given modern dress by the Yoruba narrator with the insertion of the gun for the bow and arrow and the airplane for less advanced artifacts of man.

Why the Sky Is So Far Away

The wide separation of earth and sky has always challenged the inventiveness of the primitive mind, and somewhere in nearly every culture there is a story, or perhaps a number of stories, to explain it. Among the North

American Indians, for example, is the myth that once earth and sky were united but, in a later time, were pushed apart to make room for mankind (Motif A625.2). They were thought to be the world parents of mankind: the Sky Father and the Earth Mother. In "Why the Tortoise's Shell Is Cracked and Crooked," a *pourquoi* that follows, heaven is still close enough so that earthlings can climb to it on a rope.

The Nigerian explanation is not so much a creation myth as a tale of paradise lost. Living in a golden age, men forgot God's benevolence and fell from grace. The specific offense that earns the displeasure of the Deity is here quite different from the errors of wayward man in the Hebraic-Christian and Greek traditions. In this tale, as in "The Test" (among the Moral Fables), the religious orientation is monotheistic, indicating a late date, probably, for its composition.

Of special interest is the reference to an early time when man's eyes were on his knees. Is this an appearance in the oral tradition of the same beings described by Sir Walter Raleigh as ". . . a nation of people whose heads appear not above their shoulders"? There was a fairly widespread belief among the Elizabethans in just such creatures. See Shakespeare's *The Tempest*, III, iii; and *Othello*, I, iii.

Why the Bat Comes Out Only at Night

Of all the Nigerian *pourquois,* this tale (incorporating Motifs A2491.1 and B261.1) seems to have the widest distribution, especially among the Yoruba and Ibo peoples. See, for further examples, M. I. Ogumefu, *Yoruba Legends,* p. 11; and G. T. Basden, *Among the Ibos of*

Nigeria, pp. 281ff. The Yoruba version here, told by Olawale Idewu, bears some resemblance to the Aesopean fable of the bat, the birds, and the beasts in its cast of characters and in the nature of the conflict.

The Hand and the Fingers

This particular tale, as far as we can determine, has no close parallels, either in African materials or in tales of cultures elsewhere. Motif A1311, which concerns origins of hands and feet, includes nothing which bears upon this particular point.

It is interesting to note that our informant used "third finger," "second finger," and "first finger" to refer to the digits English-speaking peoples often label "ring finger," "middle finger," and "index finger"; "ring finger" has apparently no place in Yoruba terminology. The identification of the digits in Mr. Idewu's account appeared clear enough to warrant keeping his translation of the Yoruba names for the fingers.

Why the Tortoise's Shell Is Cracked and Crooked

In one respect this *pourquoi* suggests the Open Sesame story (Type 676), of which there are a great many variants and analogues. Here, as in other African versions of the tale, the object of entering the room or cave is more often for food stored there than it is for gold. There is much in "Why the Tortoise's Shell Is Cracked and Crooked," of course, that is not part of the Open Sesame episode, but the tale ends in somewhat the same manner.

85

After the protagonist has found the entry to wealth, he is spied upon, in one way or another, by a second person who learns his secret. The good fortune of the hero is not enjoyed by the newcomer, however, for any one of numerous reasons. Usually he has forgotten the password for operating the door; he is trapped in the treasure room, and he is killed by the returning owner. Here, the interloper doesn't have the satisfaction of partaking of what the hoard has to offer. He is dropped back to earth and badly injured. And then, as a result of his ungracious remark to the helpful ants, he loses even the opportunity of having his shell repaired.

The tortoise here is most out of character, for, as many of the following tales will show, he is usually considered the wisest of the beasts in Nigeria. But his cracked shell must be accounted for in some way. The cunning of the dog may indicate that this tale originated somewhere farther south in Africa, perhaps among the Hottentots where the canines have greater prestige, the jackal being the wise creature there.

While the practice of eating old women during times of famine does not prevail in Nigeria today, it may well have been a custom of the not-too-distant past, reflected here in animal allegory. (Missionary records indicate that cannibalism existed among some minor tribes as late as the 1920's.) "Why the Tortoise's Shell Is Cracked and Crooked" is not the only Nigerian tale that refers to mother-eating among the animals; an even more popular tale including this motif is the *pourquoi* that explains why the tortoise lives alone. See Elphinstone Dayrell, *Folk Stories from Southern Nigeria, West Africa*, pp. 86–90. How widespread this practice was among primitive peoples is not definitely known, but it is clearly not something limited to Africa. It was the custom in the last century among the Fuegians, according to Charles Darwin (*The Voyage of the Beagle*, Chapter X).

Why the Fox Chases the Cock

Throughout the Old World the fox has been one of the popular characters of the folk tale, partly perhaps because of his ubiquity. How many other creatures have adapted themselves to living conditions ranging from the Arctic Circle to Capetown? He appears frequently in Indian tales of the *Panchatantra* and the *Jatakas;* at least twelve of Aesop's fables feature him; and in medieval Europe there was a whole cycle of tales about Reynard. A great trickster of the animal kingdom, the fox sometimes even matches wits with human beings, a story situation studied closely by Kaarle Krohn in his monograph, *Mann und Fuchs: drei vergleichende Märchenstudien.*

Among his animal colleagues the fox is frequently pitted against the bear (e.g., How the Bear Lost His Tail), the rabbit (several stories by Uncle Remus, notably the Tar-Baby account), and the cock, for whom Chaucer's Chauntecleer is but the best-known representative. The Yoruba explanation for the fox's pursuit of the cock makes Reynard more humane than is his wont: he is interested only in the cock's scalp!

Herskovits has edited ("Bulu Tales," *JAF*, LXII, 372) from nearby Cameroons a parallel tale, "How the Leopard Used to Be Afraid of Sheep." Here too the fiercer creature was originally afraid of the victim upon which he now commonly feeds. For African listeners, there is apparently much humor implicit in this kind of irony.

Why Apes Look Like People

The anachronisms of this story apparently do not bother the folk audiences to whom it is told. Airplanes are elements of the human scene, and so they are alluded to in the tale, though the ape is even older than the airplane's creator. The tortoise here is once again the thinker—both wise counselor and moral monitor.

Why Twins Are Valued in Serki

The birth of twins to human parents is an event so extraordinary that it always evokes strong reactions in societies not highly developed—either very favorable reactions or very unfavorable. The line between these diametrically opposed attitudes in West Africa can be drawn right down the middle of Nigeria, the Yorubas, with their Gold Coast and Guinea Coast neighbors to the west worshipping twins, and the Ibo, Niger Delta, and Cameroons tribes abhorring them.

Among the Ibos such a birth is felt to pollute the whole town, and everyone is ". . . obliged to throw away all the half-burnt firewood, the food cooked, and the water brought the previous night . . . ," according to A. G. Leonard in *The Lower Niger and Its Tribes*, p. 461. Unnatural and monstrous, the arrival of twins is considered ominous, both a harbinger and a cause of dire events to follow. In early times twins were almost invariably killed. The mother, forced to assume the guilt, was either killed or driven into the bush, there to die of exposure or be devoured by the wild beasts. In the Benin area a wealthy man might redeem his wife by providing a substitute victim, though he could not thus absolve her from guilt. See M. H. Kingsley, *West African Studies*, p. 455. Among the Ibibios in the Cross River area "twin towns" were established as refuges for such unfortunate mothers. In some instances, these towns were considered places of penance where mothers of twins might be purified; their term of quarantine in such a refuge might vary from two weeks to a year.

The Yorubas, on the other hand, have a traditional reverence for multiple births, a tradition which is the source of the twin-cult so widely distributed among New World Negroes. See Melville Herskovits' comment on this in *The Standard Dictionary of Folklore, Mythology and Legend,* edited by Maria Leach, II, 1134. Inhabitants of western Nigeria view twins as culture heroes, in much the same way early peoples of the Mediterranean basin did. See J. Rendel Harris, *The Cult of the Heavenly Twins.*

What we have here, then, in "Why Twins Are Valued in Serki" is apparently a justification of twin worship among Yorubas who live on the borders of the area where twins are hated. It is a very pointed *pourquoi*, one with special local significance.

 ## Moral Fables

While most Yoruba tales state or suggest a moral, many of them exist for other reasons as well. Each of the thirteen brief tales in this section appears to have been created solely for the moral it points. Several are close to the fables of Aesop, though the Greek collection, in turn, has analogues in the much older Oriental *Jatakas* and *Panchatantra*. Who is to say what course these tales took in their journey to Nigeria—if, indeed, they *are* imports? Where there is a similarity to Aesop, however, this fact is noted.

The Tortoise and the
Gourd of Wisdom

Although the fox is a popular character in African folk tales, he is not on the Dark Continent, as he is in Europe, the wisest of animals. From tribe to tribe various other creatures take precedence for wisdom and cunning. In southeastern Africa, it is the hare; along the Ivory and Gold Coasts, it is Anansi the Spider; among the Hottentots, the jackal. But in Nigeria, especially among the Yoruba people, the honors are carried off by the tortoise.

As a trickster (see next section) and counselor (in "Why Apes Look Like People," for example), he is the protagonist of a number of tales. Not always is he successful in his ventures, for he occasionally overreaches —as he does in the *pourquoi* explaining his cracked shell. But, win or lose, he usually assumes the role of the thinker.

In its different forms "The Tortoise and the Gourd of Wisdom" is a common tale in West Africa. Courlander adapts the tale twice in his collections for younger readers: once in *The Hat-Shaking Dance*, pp. 30–31, where Anansi the Spider is the protagonist; and once in the title story of *Terrapin's Pot of Sense*. Both of the versions used by Courlander are longer and more elaborate than the one told by Mr. Idewu. What we have here is the bare outline of the plot, without much of the motivation and without the subtle interplay of character found in the literary redactions.

The Test

This is a peculiar version of Type 841, One Beggar Trusts God, the Other the King. In the archetypal form of the tale, two beggars are given loaves of bread, the one who trusts God a plain loaf, the one who trusts the king a gold-filled loaf. Unaware of the difference, they exchange loaves, and the beggar who trusts God is thus rewarded. So popular was this *exemplum* in the Middle Ages in Europe and the Orient that Stith Thompson is reluctant to call it folklore. In Nigeria, it is clearly transmitted by an oral tradition, whatever its source.

The Yoruba version given here heightens the melodrama and, in keeping with the highly moralistic bent of Nigerian tales, makes the message very obvious. Instead of losing just a small reward, A-King-Protected-Person-Cannot-Be-Killed-By-God loses his life, and the king himself is forced to acknowledge the supremacy of the Deity. The only African analogues we have seen are much closer to the versions known in Europe and in Asia. See a Senegalese variant in Laurent Bérenger-Féraud, *Recueil de contes populaires de la Sénégambie,* pp. 145ff. Other variants told among the Hausa people of northern Nigeria can be found in A. Mischlich, *Lehrbuch der Hausa-Sprache,* pp. 135ff., and in A. J. Tremearne, *Hausa Superstitions and Customs,* pp. 183ff.

Yoruba names, like many North American Indian names, describe personal characteristics of the individual. The proper name *Olohun-iyo,* according to our informants, means "man with a sweet voice"; *Imodoye* means "wisdom combined with intelligence"; and *Efo-iye* means "his body is covered with feathers instead of hair." Thus, it is quite appropriate in "The Test" that the words *A-God-Protected-Person-Cannot-Be-Killed-By-King* should be hyphenated, for they are not merely descriptive of the man's attitude. They are his name.

The Man, the Dove, and the Hawk

Moral tags appended to traditional folk tales tend to be succinct, virtually proverbs. Here, however, as in "The Elephant and the Tortoise" and several other tales, the overelaboration of the moral is a conscious effort to clarify its significance for a Western listener.

The Bellicose Chicken

Reactions to one's image in the water find their way into a variety of folk tales. A story popular around the world (Type 34) tells how an animal—it is usually a wolf in Europe, often a hyena in Africa—seeing the moon reflected in a well, thinks it is a piece of cheese and dives repeatedly in an attempt to secure it. See, e.g., Franz Boas and C. Kamba Simango, "Tales and Proverbs of the Vandau of Portuguese South Africa," *JAF*, XXXV (1922), 151ff.

The episode related here by Olawale Idewu is an equally popular one, the creature who attacks his own image in the water (Motif J1791.5), varying with the teller and the locale. Usually thought of as humorous, belonging with numskull and noodlehead stories, the tale here is primarily didactic: a warning is ignored and the error of disobedience is fatal.

The Lion and the Goat

Of all the tales in this collection, none has more variants in Africa than does this animal fable about ingratitude (Type 155). In her unpublished but valuable doctoral dissertation on African folk tales (Indiana, 1938), May Augusta Klipple lists forty-eight versions that come from almost every tribe south of the upper Nile. The basic pattern holds firm: a judge (often the second or third judge to whom the case has been appealed) feigns ignorance of the precise way in which the ungrateful animal was freed, and he asks both plaintiff and defendant to re-enact the episode. The ingrate is left in his original predicament, and, symbolically, ingratitude is punished. The Hottentot, Shilluk, Vai, Saho, and Bambara variants are close to the European pattern: the ingrate is a serpent and the intended victim a man. The final judge is the wise creature of the area from which the tale comes: jackal, spider, hare, or tortoise. This Yoruba version is the only African example we have found in which a man is the judge.

The Lion, the Tortoise, and the Boar

The moral of this tale is an element superimposed upon the motif (B260) of Animal Warfare. Stated as it is, the moral sounds more like a literary than a folk proverb, but here, as elsewhere in this collection, the translation may be misleading. To the narrator, this maxim seemed quite

93

a commonplace observation, and it may well have been so in the idiom of his own language.

Here again, the tortoise is the thinker, for it is he who puts to a test the agreement reached by the three. Cunning leads him to invent an errand allowing him to measure the strength of his allies' intentions.

The Wasp and the Bee

This is clearly a *pourquoi,* for it explains why the wasp cannot make honey as his cousin the bee does. But there is also a clear-cut moral, implicit though it is: Patience is a virtue. The character who, in great haste, acquires only half the information he needs is a familiar figure in folk tales. Thus, in one version of the old favorite "How the Sea Became Salty," the ship captain, greedy for what the mill will grind for him, learns how to start it but not how to stop it, and the result for him is disastrous.

Three Friends and a Treasure

The reader will easily recognize here an analogue of the *exemplum* in "The Pardoner's Tale" of Geoffrey Chaucer. The ubiquity of this type (763) in the Old World illustrates how remarkably mobile is the folk tale. Ancient and probably deriving from Oriental sources, this *exemplum* appears in a popular work of fourteenth-century England, having been carried westward to Europe by anonymous yarnspinners. When was it first told on the banks of the Niger? Was it some colleague of Chaucer's Shipman or Merchant who first tried it on a Yoruba audience? Venturesome traders of their cut were by then sailing there from Italian and Portuguese ports and within another century would be establishing small posts along the west coast of Africa. Or was the tale brought overland by the forces of Islam when they swept across Africa and south to incorporate in their ranks the fierce Hausa horsemen of northern Nigeria? Whether the tale is told now among the Hausas we do not know, but it is common among the Nupes and the Fulahs, those minor tribes which live between the Hausas and the two other major groups to the south, the Yorubas and the Ibos. See René Basset, *Contes populaires d'Afrique,* pp. 185f., for a Fulah version; for a Nupe treatment, Leo Frobenius, *Atlantis: Volksdichtung und Volksmärchen Afrikas,* IX, 133f.

The Tortoise and the Hare

The only deviation here from the Aesopean parallel lies in the internal dialogue of the tortoise. In Aesop he simply accepts the challenge without deliberation; here he weighs the consequences of refusing the challenge and is also concerned about the outcome of the race.

The Tortoise and the Boar
The Tortoise and the Snake

Here we have interesting variants of Type 60, The Fox and the Crane (or Stork). In this type, the fox invites the crane to dinner and serves the soup in a shallow dish from which he can lap but from which the crane can pick nothing; the crane turns the tables by inviting the fox to a dinner at which the soup is served in a vase so narrow-necked that the guest cannot get at the fare, while the host easily dips into the vessel with his slender beak. Aesop's moral: One bad turn deserves another.

In the two Nigerian analogues (the first told by Ola-wale Idewu and the second told by Omotayo Adu) the actors, the motives, the trick, and the moral are all changed. It is only partly greed that motivates the fox in the Aesopean fable, for he is a practical joker and loves to cut a caper; the boar and the snake in the Nigerian tales seem to be merely greedy animals. In the Greek fables, both animals rely on their natural physical attributes, while in the Nigerian variants only the initiators of the contests do so. The boar and the snake use their superior bulk, but the tortoise, living up to his reputation for ingenuity, invents a device to defeat his rival; it is a matter of brawn versus brains. And the Nigerian moral is much more subtle: Man teaches man to be tall or short.

The Singing Crow
The Country Mouse and the City Mouse

These two tales are very close to those appearing in Aesop. Aesop's title for the first is usually given as "The Fox and the Crow," but the stories are substantially the same. The Yoruba version of the second fable is somewhat shortened, in that there is no mention of the city mouse's visit in the country.

Envy Can Kill

Of the various folk-tale types featuring the successful younger or youngest child, one of the most widely distributed is Type 480, The Spinning Women by the Spring. Stith Thompson notes: "It is found in almost all collections from every part of Europe, from southern and eastern Asia, from northern and central Africa, and from North and South America" (*The Folktale*, p. 126). In some cases the story has been greatly elaborated by either tellers or literary redactors.

The type follows a simple narrative line. While performing some chore, a younger child—often a stepchild but always unloved—is rewarded with great riches by a supernatural agency for her or his industry, humility, and obedience. Envious of the younger child's success and desirous of obtaining the same for her favorite child, the mother sends the favorite on the same chore. The favorite, lacking the virtues of his or her successful sibling, disobeys the directions of the god or spirit and earns assorted punishments, often death, instead of wealth.

Originally, the tale may have grown from a myth about a water deity, for water seems to be a fairly constant component of the setting. In the European versions, the younger sister drops her spindle into the well, dives in to recover it, and there beneath the surface meets the supernatural being who gives her the prescription for wealth and happiness. In many of the African versions the benevolent spirit has some vague and unexplained relationship to a pair of rivers. In one West African version each of the sisters is directed to bathe in the black river but not in the red river; the younger obeys and succeeds, while the elder sister bathes in the red river and dies. In a Hausa version from northern Nigeria the two rivers flow with honey and sour milk, both of which are tabu. The younger daughter, a stepchild, abstains from quenching her thirst in either; the elder child drinks openly from each and thereby loses the proffered reward (Tremearne, *Hausa Superstitions and Customs,* pp. 424–425). Here in the Yoruba variant, the River of Dye and the River of Blood seem to have lost their original function, whatever that function was. The informant knew only that these obstacles lay along the route.

Of ethnological interest is the mother-daughter relationship in "Envy Can Kill." Here there is no need for the stepdaughter of the European variants. The blood mothers of both daughters can be present in a tale set in a polygynous society. And the relative ages of the girls are not stated but implied: the successful girl is the daughter of the junior wife.

"Envy Can Kill," like "The Elephant and the Tortoise," below, is a choric tale or *cante fable* drawing much of its interest and suspense from the dialogue sung by various characters—in this case by the ghost-man and Alake first and then by the ghost-man and Abeo. For a number of Bantu stories utilizing this storytelling device see J. Torrend, *Specimens of Bantu Folk-Lore.*

 ## Trickster Tales

In some cultures, ranging from the Oriental to the North American Indian, the trickster is a favorite folk type. At times he is the wily and respected planner, like Ulysses; sometimes he is the *picaro,* a rascal who preys on others and lives thus by his wits; sometimes he is simply an ordinary person who exploits the opportunities that Chance puts in his way; or, finally, he may be the simpleton who succeeds in spite of himself, as the hero of the Jack Tales sometimes does. In the eight Yoruba tales of this section, the trickster appears in all these guises but the last. Nowhere else in this collection are humor and satire so evident.

Just Say "Ree"

This is an analogue of Type 1585, The Lawyer's Mad Client. Another African version can be found in a small volume by William Barker and Cecilia Sinclair, *West African Folk-Tales,* pp. 139f.

Theft is a very serious crime in Nigeria, and much rested here on the successful pleading of the case. In many areas, theft is close on the heels of murder as the most heinous of the offenses against society. (For another story involving theft, see "The Body in the Coffin" later in this section.) The hoodwinking of the lawyer is viewed by the Yoruba audience as an exploit of a trickster rather than as a moral offense. Here, as in many African groups, contractual agreements involving money are rarely considered absolutely binding unless they are made between kinsfolk.

Note also that the Crown Counsel is involved in judging this particular case of theft, suggesting that the story may have been adapted to fit colonial conditions in Africa. In Nigeria cases of theft not involving British offices and interests are ordinarily judged by native princes or kings, often following "palavers" of the community. Native judges tend to be rigorous in treatment of thieves. As recently as 1859, in Abeokuta—a place in which this tale is regularly told—the penalty for theft was extreme, being "either decapitation or foreign slavery." See Robert

NOTES

Campbell, *A Pilgrimage to My Motherland; An Account of a Journey among the Egbas and Yorubas of Central Africa in 1859–60.*

The Three Tasks

From time immemorial the suitor has been assigned diffi-cult tasks for securing his bride. The winning of Rachel by Jacob is but one of the scores of tales of this kind. Making the speechless girl speak is one such task (Type 945); making the humorless girl laugh (Motif H341) is another—this one often accomplished by parading in front of her a whole train of people helplessly stuck to-gether (Type 571). Often the person (usually the girl's father) who prescribes the labors thinks them impossible of achievement, but in spite of their difficulty the hero succeeds. The suitor sometimes receives assistance from a helpful animal, from a creature of the supernatural world, or from the prospective bride herself; or he may simply win by using his wits, as he does here in "The Three Tasks."

One of the tasks set the suitors in this story has ap-peared over a wide range of folk literature, most notably in *The Thousand and One Nights:* to tell a story that will last for a period of time far exceeding that usually required for the telling of a tale. And the device used here by the clever farmer, that of repeating the same de-tail of the rodent and the grain, dates from well before the time of Christ. But the other two tasks are peculiarly African; we have been unable to locate either one of these in any of our sources as related to European or Western lore.

The Tortoise and the Tug of War

In his *Motif Index* Thompson assigns ninety-nine numbers and their subdivisions to contests won by deception, most of them involving tests of physical strength: running, jumping, throwing, wrestling, climbing. The tug of war is a popular kind of match in many African tales, and the tiny tortoise as the trickster-winner of such a contest is common.

It is interesting to compare the tale given here with a variant in Elphinstone Dayrell's *Folk Stories from Southern Nigeria, West Africa,* in which the tortoise defeats his rivals not by pitting them against each other but by challenging them separately and then, at the crucial moment of each struggle, snubbing the rope. He pulls against the elephant from beneath the water, where he snubs the rope around a submerged rock; he pulls against the hippopotamus from the land where he simply ties the rope around a tree. In the Dayrell version, too, the tortoise wins a monetary reward (twenty thousand rods) in each contest; in this present version, the battle of wits is primary, since the tortoise reaps nothing but satisfaction.

In the Cape Verde Islands, off the west coast of Africa, the trickster is a rabbit, and the aquatic creature pitted against the elephant is a whale.

The Elephant and the Tortoise

Three common motifs go into the composition of this tale, brief as it is: the fatal deception based on flattery; the friendly bird that tries in vain to warn the victim; the illness that can be cured only with the heart of a certain beast. The eating of a heart, whether as a symbolic gesture or, as here, as a purportedly medicinal measure, plays a part in the customs and beliefs of many primitive peoples. Sometimes it is the heart of a monkey that is needed; in African tales it is more often the heart of a large and dangerous animal. Along the Gold Coast it is the leopard's heart which holds the magic remedy. See I. Bellon, "Märchen des Tschi-Volkes auf der Gold-küste," *Mitteilungen des Seminars für Orientalische Sprachen,* XVII (1914), 20ff.

This is one of three tales told by Omotayo Adu in which song constitutes a large part of the story. In the version he taped for us, each time a song is mentioned the narrator actually sings the song, in the interesting and unusual "multitonal" scale of Nigerian music. There is no satisfactory means here of notating this music, and no exact translation of the songs is available. Though the rest of the story was told in English, the songs were invariably sung in the Yoruba tongue. The story gains additional interest for the listener because of this central function of the music.

The king's bellman, or messenger, is a familiar figure in the Yoruba community. When the king has occasion to make a proclamation, to recruit soldiers or representatives, or to summon various individuals to him, he sends out his bellman, who calls the townspeople to listen to the message of the king. With him the bellman carries two bells, a large one and a small one, attached side by side and beaten alternately with quick strokes. The last three beats come on the small bell alone, and mark the end of the bell signal. Then, with due formality, the bellman greets the people in the name of the king and announces the message he has been sent to deliver. After he has completed one announcement, the bellman goes to another quarter of the village or town and repeats the bell-ringing and the announcement. An announcement made by the king's bellman can scarcely escape the attention of anyone who is within the environs of the town—thus the elephant's friend, the small bird, knew of the search for someone to procure the heart of an elephant.

There is another Yoruba tale similar to the one Omotayo Adu gives here, except that it gives a different reason for killing the elephant: he is destructive. In this version, collected by M. I. Ogumefu, the tortoise who volunteers to trap the elephant is promised the most common of rewards for heroism in the folk tale: marriage to the king's daughter (Motif T68). See his *Tales of the Tortoise*, pp. 7ff.

The Girl Who Knew the King

Tests of recognition are often required of characters in folk tales. They must, under very difficult and confusing circumstances, identify long-lost children, transformed fiancés, and assorted people traveling under a variety of disguises. Thompson assigns nearly two hundred numbers to "identity tests" of this sort. (For another example of a story involving an identity test, see "Three Wives and a Porridge" in the last section of this volume.)

The person and the face of the king in Yoruba communities have traditionally been concealed, a practice that is now slowly yielding to change. In and around Abeokuta, the area from which Olawale Idewu comes, the face of the king is not revealed to his subjects. Robert Campbell, in *A Pilgrimage to My Motherland*, written one hundred years ago, commented on this point (p. 31):

The king of Abbeokuta [sic], whose person is considered too sacred for the popular gaze, is never permitted to leave the palace except on special occasions, and then he only goes into the open space without the palace-gates, one of his wives being in attendance to screen his face with a large fan. So with the king of Oyo, who once or twice only in the year exhibits himself to the public, decorated in his best robe and wearing a crown of coral. At these times any one can stare at his majesty with impunity. In Ilorin the king may not be seen, except as a mark of special favor, even by those to whom he affords the privilege of an audience.

The claim made by the girl in this tale is thus not only open to question; it is also a serious violation of the authority and sacredness of the king's position.

This indiscretion of the heroine gets her into trouble and her innate kindness gets her out. She has befriended a palace pet who comes to her rescue in her time of need, a good example of the services rendered by Friendly Animals (Motifs B300–B599).

Here again, the songs mentioned were actually sung by Omotayo Adu in the telling of the story.

The Body in the Coffin

In the world of the folk, corpses are suspect. Will they revive? Will they turn into vampires? Are they really dead? Many a tale tells of the corpse who speaks, the corpse whose nose bleeds when his murderer passes by, the corpse which remains lifelike indefinitely. Any corpse invites conjecture, and observers are wont to divert themselves with idle speculation about it. Thus the tricksters of this Nigerian tale invite trouble when they hide their stolen goods in a coffin.

This motif (H586.5) is apparently not as common in

Africa as it is in Europe and Asia. The only other African use of it that we have seen is in "Shani and Tabak," a tale in C. H. Stigand's *Black Tales for White Children*, pp. 140ff.

The Right Recompense

In this tale of fatal deception the predator abandons all discretion in his quest for food and, like the wolf of "The Three Little Pigs," is himself cooked. The final line, with its play on words, illustrates the grim humor that one sometimes finds in primitive cultures. One is reminded of Oliver La Farge's chilling story "The Happy Indian Laughter," *New Yorker*, XXXI (August 6, 1955), 20–26.

The Lovers

The story of the returning husband who is hoodwinked (Type 1419) was a common *fabliau* of the Middle Ages. The device of the lover hidden in a vase or tub appears in The Second Story of the Seventh Day of Boccaccio's *Decameron*, though otherwise the Italian tale is different from the Yoruba.

Richard Chase recently collected almost exactly the same tale given here in Beech Creek, North Carolina, where it is known as a "step-husband" story. (A step-husband, Chase reports, is a man who steps in when the real husband is away!) See his *American Folk Tales and Songs*, pp. 43, 46–47.

A fairly close African parallel to Olawale Idewu's tale

comes from west Sudan. See Moussa Travele, *Proverbes et contes Bambara*, pp. 76f.

 ## Fertility Tales

Among the Yorubas the desire for children is especially strong, due in part, perhaps, to the peculiar demands of their patrilineal society: women who produce children are held in esteem, and it is considered a reproach for a married woman to be childless. Add to this condition the fact of the extremely high Nigerian infant mortality rate (aggravated, ironically, by brutal obstetrical practices), and one can quite readily appreciate the almost obsessive preoccupation of women and their husbands with the question of fertility.

Here, resort to divinities of fecundity to procure offspring is both natural and reasonable. By the employment of various rites—vows, prayers, and offerings—women put their trust in Ifa (the god of fecundity) and Orisha-Oko (the god of the farm and of crops in general, who is also concerned with human fertility). That their confidence is not misplaced is witnessed both by the survival of the custom and by its frequent recounting in native tales. In one of the following tales, "The Promise," Orisha-Oko answers an appeal and subsequently insists upon the promised sacrifice, a suitable conclusion for what is quite a usual and satisfactory arrangement.

Resort is also had to potions of various types, with or without appeal to a god of fecundity. The use of a magical porridge or medicine in each of the tales in this section is followed by conception. When we asked our informants, both biology students, how such substances could be effective, they maintained that they did not know *how,* but that it *was true:* such a procedure consistently produced the desired result.

Most of the tales of magic remedies for barrenness and impotence (Motif T591.1) have been recorded outside Africa, however—most often among Irish, Jewish, and East Indian peoples.

The Promise

Tree spirits or tree gods are widely considered to have the power of making women fruitful. (See Frazer, *The Golden Bough,* for comment on this point.) The teller of the tale "The Promise," Omotayo Adu, believes that the tree commonly held propitious for childbearing by women in his area is the mahogany. Both Omotayo Adu and Olawale Idewu indicated that this practice of securing aid from tree gods in the matter of ensuring childbirth exists among the Yorubas currently, and that it appears to produce the desired result.

A woman approaching the tree god on this errand is accompanied by a priest, who intercedes for the woman. After the woman herself has petitioned and has promised a sacrifice of an appropriate kind to the tree god on the birth of her child, she is furnished a medicine by the priest. This she takes, and in due course of time she is delivered of a child. She is then bound to take to the tree god the sacrifice she has promised him.

In Yoruba legend there is a notable instance of a rash promise made by a woman to a deity, one that cost her heavily to pay. Moremi, a woman of great beauty and virtue, undertook to deliver her countrymen, the Yorubas, from the terrible, devastating raids brought upon them by their enemies, the Ibos, during their early days at Ile Ife. She vowed to the deity of the Esinmirin stream that she would offer him the highest sacrifice she could afford if he would assist her in carrying out her plan successfully. At great risk of her life, she was at last able to bring about the destruction of the Ibos and the end of their raids upon her people. She thereupon went to the Esinmirin stream to honor her vow to the deity. She offered a goat, a ram, and then a bullock, but the god would not accept these as sacrifices. She then found out from the priests that the only sacrifice the god would accept was her only son, Olurogbo, and, true to her vow, she gave her son to the deity. For this meeting of her vow she was greatly honored by her people.

Three Wives and a Porridge

As was mentioned in the note for "The Girl Who Knew the King," identity tests are very common in folk literature. The particular test in the story "Three Wives and a Porridge" rests on a folk belief in the intuitive power of the child to recognize his own kin (Motif H175).

The Man and the Fertility Porridge
The Tortoise and the
Forbidden Porridge

Among the impossibilities accepted as quite matter-of-fact in the world of the folk tale is male pregnancy. Examples of this motif (T578) are found among the Irish, Icelandic, Scandinavian, and Eskimo tales. For a North American Indian tale that uses it see Robert J. Miller, "Situation and Sequence in the Study of Folklore," *JAF*, LXV (1952), 36. In Africa the motif has been recorded among the Basuto people as well as among the Yorubas.

Supplementary
Notes

In the first edition of *Nigerian Folk Tales*, the Notes afforded an opportunity for readers to assess the Idewu and Adu tales in the light of variants from other oral traditions; references were made wherever possible to types and motifs in the indexes then available. The Supplementary Notes, on the contrary, consider solely Yoruba variants for selected tales from *Nigerian Folk Tales*. No consideration has been given here to the many types and hundreds of motifs clearly evident in the variants; such information has been reserved for some future in-depth study of Yoruba tales.

For convenience, short titles have been used for the volumes cited, with the full titles and publication data for these works furnished in the Bibliography. Special note should be taken of two bilingual studies cited, Bascom's *Ifa Divination* and LaPin's unpublished three-volume dissertation. All of the Ifa divination verses (in which the variants cited are incorporated) are furnished by Bascom in Yoruba as well as in English, with the matching texts on facing pages; the English text is just half the length indicated by the inclusive page references. Almost all of LaPin's tales are furnished both in Yoruba and in English, with the matching texts on successive pages; as in Bascom's volume, the LaPin English texts are only half as long as the inclusive page references would suggest. (Both Bas-com's and LaPin's works utilize tonal markings on Yoruba words and proper names, but we have not provided tonal markings here although we are well aware of their significance in Yoruba communication.)

Space does not permit summaries of the variants, but enough indication of the content and style of each one is given to direct readers to the variants most appropriate for their individual pursuits. All of the variants cited seem to us to have value for what they reflect of the translators' tastes and biases and authorial styles as well as for what they reveal of Yoruba verbal art. The Yoruba themselves recognize at least two major kinds of oral narratives: the *itan*, or story without song, used to furnish direct, straightforward accounts of origins, battles, religious in-stitutions, and the acts of gods and of great men—tales to be told in the daytime and to be believed—and the *alo*, or story with a song or songs integral to the plot, understood to be enjoyable and instructive but not accepted as true, told in the evening, and used largely for entertainment and as fare for children. Non-Yoruba translators and adapters of Yoruba tales for the most part either have been unaware of these distinctions or have been satisfied to ignore them. They have thus published versions of the *alo*, for example, either entirely without reference to the song or songs upon which it depends, with only one or two uses of the song or songs (often wrenched into Western cadence and supplied with end-rhymed lines), or with squinting reference to the songs included in the in situ telling ("as he pursued her he sang that he would tear her in small pieces, and she in an-other song replied that he would never overtake her" [Ogumefu, "The Leopard-Man," p. 19]). Repetition of the songs delights Yoruba listeners, but reproduction of the songs constitutes a chore for many translators and adapters, and as a result the songs have been given little or no attention in the second-language versions. Absence of or truncation of the songs, omission of the puns and other forms of word play, substitution of Western patterns for the traditional opening and closing formulas, and use of Western terms for Yoruba foods, material objects, and natural phenomena have blurred the image of the genuine Yoruba oral narrative. Also, reduction or entire omission of dialogue, lack of evidence of audience participation, and the limitations of print have robbed the translated versions of the dramatic performance characteristic of Yoruba storytelling. Still, translations and adaptations provide the Western non-Yoruba-speaking reader with his only access to Yoruba folktales; though shorn of Yoruba art and drama, the second-language variants provide sufficiently valid content to be useful in a lay approach to Yoruba narratives.

The Hunter and the Deer

Yoruba variants readily available for comparison include "The Beautiful Girl and the Fish" (pp. 13–16) and "The Hunter and the Hind" (pp. 77–82) in Fuja's *Fourteen Hundred Cowries*, Verse 153–1 (pp. 374–85) in Bascom's *Ifa Divination*, and "The Deer-Woman of Owo" (pp. 150–54) in Courlander's *Tales of Yoruba Gods and Heroes*. These variants offer significant differences from Olawale Idewu's version.

In "The Beautiful Girl and the Fish," the fish-husband is killed by the girl's outraged father, and the distraught mortal wife, told that she has eaten some of her husband's flesh, plunges into the river from which her otherworldly mate had come and is thereupon transformed into a mer-

113

maid. In "The Hunter and the Hind," the hind-wife, accepted by the other wives but overwhelmed by longing for her natural life in the bush, finds the hidden hind-skin, reassumes her hind form, and flees; the hunter, banished to the bush for this unnatural marriage, dies many years later, "completely alone and uncared for." In "The Deer-Woman of Owo," the otherworldly wife, taunted by her cowives, is taken into the sky under the protection of Olorun [God], but she becomes a benefactor to the town because her mortal husband has been good to her; annual sacrifices to her ensure her continued patronage. In Verse 153–1, the otherworldly wife, initially a buffalo, after being taunted by the senior wife and directed to her buffalo hide, soaks the hide until it will fit her, kills the senior wife with her horns, and leaves one horn to which sacrifices are to be offered annually for the well-being of the hunter's household.

The Christian orientation that prompted Idewu's veiled condemnation of polygamy is not echoed in any of the variants cited; the moral appended to "The Hunter and the Hind" ("Be content with what you possess, for by seeking what is strange you may end by losing all."), found in other contexts in the Yoruba oral tradition, has in Idewu's version yielded to the forces of acculturation. The widespread practice of sacrifice among the Ifa and other cults accounts for the conclusions of two of the variants; both offer explanations for the origin of recognized sacrificial customs. In the four variants, as well as in the Idewu tale, community rejection of "unnatural" matings reflects the value system both of the Yoruba narrators and of their audiences.

None of the variants examined appears to us to suggest either the drama or the poignancy present in the version told by Olawale Idewu.

114

The Hunter and the Witch

The published Yoruba versions of this particular tale are more numerous than are those for any other narrative told by Idewu. The emphasis placed—at least, until recently—among the Yoruba on the responsibility of the families in arranging marriages for the young and the disastrous consequences visited on young men or women who obstinately choose their own mates are readily apparent in the oral tradition. We have selected for comment eleven of the available variants: "Motinu and the Monkeys" (pp. 44–49) and "The Hunter and His Magic Flute" (pp. 155–61) in Fuja's *Fourteen Hundred Cowries;* an untitled tale (pp. 267–69) in Ellis's *The Yoruba-Speaking Peoples;* Verse 175–1 (pp. 416–23) in Bascom's *Ifa Divination;* "Jäger und Schlangenfrau" (pp. 233–38) in Frobenius's *Atlantis,* Volume 10; "The Leopard-Man" (pp. 68–71) and "The Head" (pp. 96–103) in Baumann's *Ajapa the Tortoise;* "The Leopard-Man" (pp. 18–20) and "The Head" (pp. 38–40) in Ogumefu's *Yoruba Legends;* and two tales from Volume 3 of LaPin's unpublished dissertation, "The Girl Who Married a Python" (pp. 442–48) and "A Girl Marries a Monkey" (pp. 679–92).

In most of these variants, a beautiful girl who has refused many eligible suitors is attracted to a handsome stranger in the marketplace and, determined to marry him, follows him home despite his warnings that she will regret her action. The stranger proves to be either an animal in temporary human form or a disembodied head that has borrowed the body parts necessary to complete his figure and must return those parts as he goes home with his increasingly horrified bride. A few variants present a

115

young man as similarly deceived by a beautiful young female stranger; these latter variants are somewhat closer to
Idewu's tale than are the others, but all of them hold in
common the condemnation of hasty and ill-advised marital
choice.

Ogumefu's and Baumann's versions of "The Leopard-
Man" and of "The Head" may well have come from a single source: they are almost identical in their characters,
circumstances, plots, and conclusions—though Ogumefu's
tellings are spare, while Baumann's are elaborate and include much peripheral material—with one startling exception. In keeping with her subtitle, *A Book of Nigerian
Fairy Tales*, Baumann in "The Head" has the unlucky
bride ask for similar dismemberment so that she can live
happily as a head with her husband's people—a request
that is speedily granted—and ends her tale thus: "The
moral of this story is, that where we cannot alter our
circumstances, it is the wisest course to adapt ourselves
to them." Neither Ogumefu's nor Baumann's versions
attempt to communicate the dramatic quality of Yoruba
tale-telling, nor do they include echoes of Yoruba speech
patterns or word play. Even the content is distorted in
Baumann's versions by her overblown descriptions, out of
keeping with traditional Yoruba narration. One taste of
her style may be sufficient: "let her walk by his side
through the long, dim, green paths of the forest, where
strange birds and gorgeous butterflies passed them, and the
scent of the sweetest flowers filled all the air" (pp. 69–70).

The most direct and to us most satisfying of the "head"
variants is the untitled one in Ellis's volume. It begins in
the traditional style—"My *alo* is about a woman named
Adun"—and hews to the line of Yoruba values by having
Adun at least "[show her chosen husband] to her mothers.
Her mothers said, 'Very well, go with him.' " En route

with Adun to his "distant country," the "person" returns his borrowed limbs and body, and, once home, sets Tortoise to watch Adun lest she run away. After several fruitless attempts at escape, Adun goes "to ask the *babalawo* what she should do" (p. 268). By following the witch doctor's advice, Adun is able to return home. The use of local terms and expressions ("I am going to relieve nature," *babalawo*, and *ekurus* [white-bean cakes]) and of dialogue at strategic points in the action enables Ellis to communicate at least some of the flavor of Yoruba tale-telling.

In two of the variants—"Motinu and the Monkeys" and "A Girl Marries a Monkey"—both the plots and the narrative styles are vastly different from one another. Motinu is approached by the handsome stranger, goes with him without consulting her family, does her best to please her monkey-husband and his family, and is at last rescued by a hunter, whom she eventually marries; when the monkey-husband comes again in disguise to the market, Motinu identifies him, and he is enslaved by the chief and is thus unable to return to his monkey form. Fuja employs sufficient dialogue to maintain the reader's interest and involvement, but he falls short of suggesting the drama that invests traditional tale-telling with its primary appeal. On the other hand, LaPin's male narrator interacts constantly with his audience, and his use of language—very free and quite coarse in translation—is unquestionably as close an approximation of folk narration as it is possible to confine to print. In this second tale, the young woman pursues the handsome stranger doggedly, despite his demurrals and explicit descriptions of the dreadful future that awaits her as his wife; she is unspeakably abused by her monkey-husband, and the hunter who at her pleading carries her home refuses contemptuously to marry her, despite her parents' open bribes. A comparison of these two variants provides

117

the forewarned reader with a sound sense of the degree of individualized style allowed a Yoruba storyteller. (The female narrator of "The Girl Who Married a Python" presents in a much more restrained manner a similar tale: the girl pursues the handsome stranger despite his warnings, is horrified when he throws his belongings into the river and proceeds to swallow her, and pleads in song that a nearby hunter rescue her. The hunter at last shoots the python, releasing the girl, but when he takes the girl home he insists that she sing her song, exposing her to public ridicule and rejection. She "finally died, alone." The lengthy moral points up a girl's obligation to marry a man of her parents' choosing.)

The last three variants (Ifa Verse 175–1, "The Hunter and His Magic Flute," and "Jäger und Schlangenfrau") have several important elements in common. They all concern hunters deceived by dangerous creatures or spirits disguised as beautiful women, and each of the hunters already has a wife; the tales all include life-and-death combat between the hunters and the beautiful women in their true forms (a tree-spirit, the many-mouthed sister of the Mother of the Forest, and a powerful snake); they all contain a tree of refuge; they all include three hunting dogs with names suggestive of the dogs' behavior or service; in all of the tales, the hunting dogs are summoned from a distance and rescue their masters by destroying the evil adversaries. As might be expected in Yoruba narration, each tale also has some significant differences from the others, marking it as a work of oral art as well as of oral tradition.

Of the last three variants, the Ifa Verse tale is shortest and least dramatic, as is appropriate for Yoruba sacred narratives; the tale from Frobenius is the richest of the three in flavor, in dialogue, and in its suggestion of drama. "The Hunter and His Magic Flute" is diluted in tale-telling effectiveness because of the many cultural details provided for non-Yoruba readers, because of its limited dialogue, and because of the cerebration and introspection ascribed to the hunter, essentially a man of action. The three provide an excellent set for the identification of storytelling techniques as well as for the study of motifs—a matter not considered in these Supplementary Notes, but well worth exploring.

The Hunter Who Was King

The three Yoruba variants of this tale selected for consideration differ widely among themselves and from Olawale Idewu's version both in style and in details, but all four hold in common the core of the tale: a poverty-stricken man through some agency outside himself suddenly becomes the ruler of a town, but there is one taboo that he must observe; after a period of joy and satisfaction, he violates the taboo and is immediately returned to his original hopeless state, made even more miserable by his awareness that he alone has been responsible for his loss. The lesson at the heart of all four versions is the high cost of disobedience.

In the most entertaining and unusual of the three variants ("Tortoise and His Strange Adventures," originally an *alo* but not furnished with the songs), included in Itayemi and Gurrey's *Folk Tales and Fables* (pp. 87–92), the parallel to the present tale occurs as the seventh and final episode in a series of efforts by Tortoise to gain food during a famine. Sold at last as a slave to a woman in the town of No-Men, Tortoise finds himself petted and pampered, and all the women of the town become his private harem. Only one thing is prohibited to him as king: he must not

119

climb a certain tree. Eventually, Tortoise, determined to climb that forbidden palm tree, discovers that as he descends the tree he becomes a female. Repeated attempts, each with the same alarming result, lead Tortoise to the town's secret: one by one, each of the men who had come had at last climbed the forbidden tree, and thus all had become women. In a desperate effort to conceal his change in sex, Tortoise refuses to be bathed, feigning illness, until the women suspect the truth, give him a bath by force, and reveal the consequence of his disobedience. Since Tortoise is no longer needed—he has fathered sons as well as daughters—he is beaten and thrown out, "to die of shame and of his wounds" (p. 92).

Each of the other two variants—"Olode the Hunter Becomes an Oba," in Courlander's *Olode* (pp. 32–36), and "The Disobedient Hunter," in LaPin's dissertation (Volume 3, pp. 476–84)—presents a hunter (in "Olode" one too poor even to have a wife and in "The Disobedient Hunter" one accompanied by his several wives and children) who, in desperate plight, encounters the King of the Bush (or, in LaPin's variant, the elephant, the last in a series of animals sought as prey) and, ordered to lay aside all clothing and weapons, enters a huge tree (or, in LaPin's variant, remains with eyes closed for five minutes) and finds himself (and, in LaPin's version, his family) in a town expecting the arrival of a new *oba* (king, or chief). Each is treated royally, given sway over the entire town and its people, and lives richly. But each must observe an accepted taboo: Olode must not open the carved door in the third house; the other hunter must not open the door of a certain small house (although he is handed the key to that door!). Each hunter rules well and then—in both instances because of drunken insolence—opens the forbidden door and finds himself (and his family, also, in LaPin's variant) destitute outside the Eden that he had experienced.

The styles of the four versions are helpful indicators of the Yoruba narrators' freedom to handle a single traditional tale in highly individual fashions. Each has its merits, and all are well worth reading in entirety. The Courlander version appears the most "literary" of the four, with its deliberate effort to suggest Yoruba diction but with authorial intrusions to provide non-Yoruba readers with sociological information; in its attempt to reach both ends of the spectrum, it fails to transmit a sense of dramatic performance.

Why the Bat Comes Out Only at Night

Of the three variants selected for this tale—"Why the *Ajao* [large bat] Remained Unburied" in Ellis's *The Yoruba-Speaking Peoples* (pp. 252–53), "The Bat" in Ogumefu's *Yoruba Legends* (p. 17), and "The Bat" in Baumann's *Ajapa the Tortoise* (pp. 51–52)—none includes any "animals" other than rats, none includes any statement by the bat himself citing evidence that he is a bird (or an animal) by virtue of certain physical characteristics, and only the latter two involve a battle in which the bat fights first on one side and then on the other.

Ellis's variant departs from the majority of the published explanations for the isolation of the bat in eschewing the "battle" plot and presenting instead the socially significant question of which "relatives" (the birds or the rats) should undertake the responsibility of providing proper burial for the dead *ajao*. First the birds, seeing that *ajao* lacks feathers, refuse to perform the funeral ceremonies; then the rats, observing that *ajao* has no tail, reject him as a family member and refuse to bury him. The tale is not treated as a *pourquoi*. Despite the story's brevity, its abundant dialogue at critical turns and the poignancy of the situation heighten the drama of its telling and make it both satisfying and memorable.

The tale held in common by Ogumefu and Baumann pits the birds against the rats in battle, with Bat choosing to support the rats until victory for the birds appears certain; without explanation or apology, Bat then forsakes the rats for the birds. At this point, the narratives diverge from one another: In Ogumefu's telling, the rats and the birds, "disgusted at this cowardly action," combine their forces and attack the bat, necessitating his coming out thereafter only at night. In Baumann's rather wordy and sentimentalized version—"Poor Bat was now sorry for the way he had acted, but it was too late, and ever since then he has been shunned by all creatures . . ." (p. 52)—the birds and the rats remain enemies of one another, but both groups condemn Bat as a traitor. In both Ogumefu and Baumann, the tale is presented as a *pourquoi* accounting for the bat's nocturnal habits. As is Olawale Idewu's version, they are in keeping with the primary Yoruba explanation for this phenomenon.

Why the Tortoise's Shell Is Cracked and Crooked

Of the six variants discussed here, only three are close to Olawale Idewu's tale. In "Antelope's Mother: the Woman on the Moon," from Courlander's *Olode the Hunter* (pp. 72–76), a three-way *pourquoi* is offered: why Tortoise's shell is cracked, why cockroaches are flat, and why the moon has a figure (an antelope) visible on it. As in Idewu's tale, the famished animals agree to kill their own mothers as food to sustain their own lives. Antelope, determined not to kill his mother, takes her to the moon for safety (food is plentiful there), and cooks a well-seasoned rotten-wood substitute for her flesh. When Antelope sings a certain song, his mother lets down a rope from the moon that he can ascend in order to be fed; wily Tortoise eventually extracts this secret from Antelope and reports it to the king (the lion). Sent on an errand by the king, Antelope returns to find many animals—including the king himself—clinging to the rope and already halfway to the moon. In response to Antelope's altered song, his mother cuts the rope and the animals fall, some to their deaths and the others badly injured. Tortoise, dissatisfied with the speed at which the cockroaches are putting his broken shell together, beats them until they become flat; the cracks in Tortoise's shell are still visible today; too, Antelope's mother can still be seen on the moon.

"The Wise Dog" (pp. 119–24) in Fuja's *Fourteen Hundred Cowries* employs the dog as the one creature who spares his mother but has the dog tell the tortoise about his secret source of food. Subsequently, many animals, including the king (the lion), struggle to ride on the "tiny bench" and on the attached rope to be lifted by Dog's mother to "Heaven" for food. When Dog's mother, detecting the cheat, cuts the rope, all fall and are killed except the tortoise, saved by his shell. The shell is not pictured as broken and then patched; instead, the tortoise is beheaded for having caused the death of the king of the animals. The *pourquoi*'s conclusion explains both why Dog relies on man to feed him and why Dog never tells his secrets. The style and the vocabulary of this version are farther removed from the Yoruba traditional patterns than they are in most of Fuja's tellings; still, the core of the tale has not been lost.

Volume 2 of LaPin's dissertation (pp. 112–26) offers in

SUPPLEMENTARY NOTES

"Tortoise and Lo'tun" a narrative that is in several ways the most satisfactory variant found for Idewu's tale. In its style and structure it is close to both the content and the drama of traditional Yoruba storytelling. A familiar formulaic opening is used:

> "Here is an *alo*."
> "Alo *it is!*" [Audience]
> "My *alo* snaps and falls *fiririri*
> It lands heavily *gboo*
> It strikes elsewhere *paa*
> And finally falls on the head of Lo'tun.

To protect his mother while the others, famished, are killing their mothers for food, Lo'tun builds her a new house "in heaven," offering as a substitute for his mother's flesh bits of rotted wood and leftovers from "his earlier portions." His grateful mother lets down a rope which Lo'tun climbs for food in that place of plenty. (The song he sings to call his mother is furnished each time.) Tortoise encounters Lo'tun, persuades him that he has lost all his "tricks" and is thus reliable, and participates in Lo'tun's next visit to his mother. Tortoise conceals portions of all the foods served, and as soon as he has reached the earth again, he produces the fragments he has hidden and promises to take the other animals there to see for themselves. They gather, and Tortoise (in a nasal voice that is puzzling to Lo'tun's mother but characteristic of Tortoise) sings Lo'tun's song. The rope descends, and the animals begin to climb. Lo'tun, arriving "when there were only about four knots to go," sings to his mother to let go of the rope, and watches as the animals fall. Lo'tun kills those whose fall has not destroyed them, but since he cannot kill Tortoise because of that heavy shell, he flogs him again and again. Though Tortoise's broken shell is patched by Cockroach, Ant, and Stink Ant, Tortoise displays his "thankfulness" by pulling out Cockroach's intestine, snipping Ant's body until he becomes very small, and flattening Stink Ant's head. LaPin's narrator closes the tale in a traditional fashion: "That is the end of my *alo*. I toss it behind me so the rain torrent will carry it away."

Two other variants offer widely different explanations for Tortoise's scarred shell. Ellis's untitled tale (pp. 271–74) in *The Yoruba-Speaking Peoples* traces Tortoise's markings to his being "smashed" by the owner of a yam plantation after Tortoise's greed has led him to overload himself with stolen yams and thus made him unable to escape before the owner's return (also, the yams are hidden in a rock that opens and closes on verbal command; the lizard knows the words and manages to escape, while the tortoise is unable to imitate his informant in this trick). Tortoise's shell is mended, at his request, by the cockroach and the ant, but the mends still show. On the other hand, Verse 166–1 in Bascom's *Ifa Divination* attributes the marks on Tortoise's shell to the scratches made by Leopard, enraged that Tortoise has stolen his drum to play at a dance given by the King of the Sky. (The portion of the verse relating the theft of Leopard's drum—sometimes by the monkey and sometimes by some other creature—and the anxiety felt in turn by various innocent suspects occurs in a number of Yoruba folktales, chiefly in *pourquoi* narratives explaining the appearance or behavior of certain animals [why the monkey lives in trees, for example].)

The sixth variant, drawn from Volume 3 of LaPin's dissertation (pp. 498–508) and titled "The Younger Generation Revolts," bears similarity to Idewu's tale only in the circumstance that all the young men in a town kill their fathers so that the sons can become officials in their stead. The *babalawo*'s son hides his father, whose subsequent wise solutions to the new *oba*'s three riddling and ridiculous demands lead to the identification of the old *babalawo* and his elevation to the post of elder adviser to the *oba*.

Though the *pourquoi* element is strong in several of the six versions, and though the conclusions seem to vary one from another, one trait appears to be extolled both in four of the variants and in Idewu's narration: the wisdom of moderation.

Why Apes Look Like People

Courlander's "The Medicine of Olu-Igbo," in his *Tales of Yoruba Gods and Heroes* (pp. 171–73), bears marked resemblance to Olawale Idewu's tale. In answer to the pleading of both wild and domestic animals, Olu-Igbo, "the supreme spirit of the bush," makes a medicine that will transform the animals so that they will all "look like men and live like men." The monkey, excluded from their deliberations but suspecting a consultation with Olu-Igbo, hurries ahead and, hidden in a tree, observes all the preparations. When the magic medicine (*juju*) has been prepared but before the animals can rub their bodies with the *juju*, the monkey throws a branch that breaks the bowl filled with the precious medicine; at the same time, he imitates the call of a human hunter. Frightened, the rest of the animals flee, and the monkey rubs what is left of the spilled *juju* on his hands, his face, and his buttocks. "By his transformed hands, face, and buttocks, the bush creatures understood that the monkey had been at the gathering and obtained some of the juju" (p. 173).

The premature rejoicing evidenced by the to-be-transformed animals in Idewu's tale is absent in Courlander's variant; it occurs widely in Yoruba tales otherwise unrelated to this one—for example, in Fuja's "The Sad Story of the Tadpole" (pp. 17–19 in his *Fourteen Hundred Cowries*), in which the tadpole, told by the frogs that he is to be made their new king, orders a seven-day celebration prior to the crowning, drinks too much, falls while showing off his ability at dancing and breaks a leg, and is not crowned king after all because no deformed person can be crowned king of the frogs. The moral appended to this variant serves equally well all three versions of the tale— Idewu's, Courlander's, and Fuja's: "When you hear of a good thing coming your way, take care of yourself."

Why Twins Are Valued in Serki

We have been unable to find any even remotely appropriate Yoruba variants for this tale. In view of the continued strong feeling among the Yoruba concerning twins, however, we wish to comment on three tales offering useful insights into the folk-narrative uses of the concept of twinship. Courlander's *Tales of Yoruba Gods and Heroes* (pp. 141–45) furnishes an account of the origin of twins that views them as sent initially into the world as *abiku* (children born to die very young) to avenge the relentless killing of monkeys by a certain hunter; when the hunter, after repeated consultation of seers, abandons his killing of monkeys, his wife bears twins who are able to live and thrive. The style in Courlander's telling is matter-of-fact and thus carries little or no suggestion of Yoruba tale-telling flavor, but the passage includes some informative observations about the naming and treatment of twins.

A vastly different account is furnished in Ogumefu's

SUPPLEMENTARY NOTES

"The Twin Brothers" (pp. 33–36 of her *Yoruba Legends*). At a time when twins are still abhorred among the Yoruba, twin sons born to a Yoruba king are removed with their mother to a place of safety. Subsequently, the king dies, and the two young men—told of their royal origin by their mother prior to her own death—determine by lot that the younger one will become the new king and then will send for his brother. But the elder brother, after enjoying for a time the honor of being the king's brother, becomes jealous and determines to gain the crown for himself; he therefore drowns his twin and, feigning grief, becomes king. The crime is revealed first to the usurper by a fish at the very place of the drowning; though the murderer kills the fish, the crime is revealed a second time—in the presence of the courtiers—by the waves of the river itself (in each instance, the revelation is included in a song, provided in the text). When a search confirms the accusation, the usurper is rejected, whereupon he takes poison and dies. Ogumefu's version is clearly a truncated form of the traditional one; also, the use of such terms as "courtiers" and "nobles" and the intrusion of descriptions of the royal umbrella and other court paraphernalia reduce the validity of this variant as a reflection of Yoruba narration. The tale seems useful to us primarily because it presents the other side of the coin of twinning shown in Idewu's version.

The third variant, "The Twins," in Fuja's *Fourteen Hundred Cowries* (pp. 50–67), is entirely different from all three of the other narratives. In Fuja's tale, two separate sets of adventures are experienced by the principals; life tokens, magic gifts, medicines for resuscitation and for protection against witchcraft, identification of the king through gifts given to his dog and his cat, a dragon-slaying episode, and huge natural objects created as memorials to the twins' parents combine to make a folktale that in its local setting and dramatic presentation must surely have found a responsive audience. Even on the printed page, the narrative comes alive sufficiently to suggest the power and creativity of Yoruba verbal art.

The Tortoise and the Gourd of Wisdom

Itayemi and Gurrey quote as a headnote to their presentation of Tortoise tales in *Folk Tales and Fables* the following traditional Yoruba opening for a Tortoise *alo:*

> My tale falls on Tortoise. It falls with a crack, and it falls on Tortoise; it falls with a thud, and still falls on Tortoise. It falls in short bits, and I lay them on my shoulder, and it falls in long bits and I put them in the basket, but it still falls on Tortoise, who is worthy enough to be the husband of Yanrinbo the Beetle.

Such an opening prepares Yoruba listeners for another tale about that clever, greedy, sly, mischievous folk hero often termed "the bald-headed elf." An awareness of the flavorful opening for such a tale should also alert the reader to expect a tale in which the Yoruba play out through Tortoise and his actions their genuine concerns for wisdom, for honesty, and for fair play.

Of the many available Yoruba variants of Idewu's story, we have selected three for discussion: "Tortoise and the Wisdom of the World" (pp. 92–93 in Itayemi and Gurrey's *Folk Tales and Fables*), "Tortoise and the World's Wisdom" (pp. 72–74 in Baumann's *Ajapa the Tortoise*), and "Tortoise and the Wisdom of the World" (pp. 972–74 of LaPin's dissertation, Volume 3). Two summaries worth mentioning are furnished by Courlander in his *Tales of Yoruba Gods and Heroes* (p. 180) and by Wonodi in his journal article, "The Role of Folk Tales in African Society."

As in Idewu's tale, Tortoise's flaw in reasoning is detected in Itayemi and Gurrey's narrative by a man (a hunter), who laughs at Tortoise's ingenuousness and advises him to hang the gourd *behind* him if he wishes to get to the top of the tree. An element absent in Idewu's version but present in many others is included in Itayemi and Gurrey's telling: the wisdom scattered from Tortoise's broken pot becomes available to everybody "throughout the world," and "anyone can still find a little bit of it if they [sic] search hard enough." This version also indicates that Tortoise planned to sell the wisdom he had gathered, and supplies details about the methods used to cork the gourd and to prepare the gourd for suspension from Tortoise's neck, suggesting that a non-Yoruba audience was anticipated for the book.

Baumann's variant identifies Tortoise's son as the one who watches the tree-climbing spectacle and then advises his father to hang the pot behind him; in this telling, following Tortoise's dropping of the gourd and the wisdom's being scattered "far and wide," Baumann concludes: "And that is why fragments of wisdom are now to be found all over the earth." This variant includes several extraneous elements that demonstrate the storyteller's freedom to innovate: the unwelcome inquiry by Tortoise's wife, the comment that gathering all the world's wisdom "took him quite a number of years," and his consideration of and rejection of two alternative methods of safeguarding the gourd of wisdom (burying it in the earth and sinking it in the sea) before his determination of the tall tree as the safest hiding place. Such details are amusing but distracting, and they appear to be confined to this particular telling.

130

Here they seem to abuse, rather than use, the storyteller's prerogative to alter a tale to taste: they lengthen the tale but do not strengthen it for oral use.

LaPin's version names Snail as the one who observes Tortoise's impractical approach to the problem of carrying the gourd up the tree, a selection well within the range of Yoruba oral-narrative possibilities in view of the Snail's role as a clever fellow capable of outthinking Tortoise. Changes due to acculturation are evidenced in this version in the use of "that would mean . . . pay him for it first," "from about eight in the morning until two in the afternoon," and "he'd stash it away." The spirited dialogue and evidence of the narrator's use of mime and of his interaction with the audience—"the wisdom rested on his front like this . . ." is one instance—communicate the performance element present in genuine Yoruba tale-telling.

The Lion, the Tortoise, and the Boar [Boa]

Despite the pace and the pressure of contemporary urban life among the Yoruba, the oral tradition refuses to die. A good case in point is the present tale. According to Chief Oludare Olajubu in "The Yoruba Singers of Tales," page 13, a variant of this tale incorporating a fourth animal has become very popular in Nigeria as a tale-song. Sung as recently as August 1979 on television and radio programs and available in phonograph and tape recordings, this tale-song combines all the "aesthetic devices of Yoruba poetry and folktale narration" (p. 11) and serves the multiple functions of entertaining, of pleasing, of teaching, and of preserving a portion of the oral tradition that might otherwise be lost. The singer, Dauda Epo Akara, has titled his song [in English translation] "Four Animals Who

Wanted to Know Each Other's 'Don'ts.' " By the use of characterization, setting, structure, content, language, and storytelling technique, Akara's song and many others of these tale-songs encourage the dissemination and retention of genuine Yoruba narratives in an urban situation uncongenial to traditional fireside tale-telling.

Presentation of the narrative as a tale-song does not sound its death knell as a spoken tale. One variant of the story, "Why the Lion, the Vulture, and the Hyena Do Not Live Together," appears in attractive dress in Courlander's *Olode the Hunter* (pp. 54–57). The presence of the hyena in the dramatis personae suggests that the tale may have traveled south and west to reach the Yoruba, but the point of the narrative is very close to that made in Idewu's tale: "[T]o state one's dislike is to initiate one's annoyance." Courlander's version is in more than one sense "literary." It begins and ends with the concept of sharing meat, admittedly a lively concern among river-forest peoples, but also a splendid "envelope-style" arrangement for a written work. The sentence structure itself—for example, "Your words, I have heard them"— and the plentiful use of dialogue are conscious efforts to recreate an oral telling. The inclusion of the provocative detail that the vulture is cooking over a fire proves, too, to be a literary necessity—though all three of the creatures in this variant normally eat their meat raw, *some* embers must be introduced in order to burn away the vulture's crest.

The pattern in Courlander's variant is quite similar to that found in Idewu's tale: the hyena, who resents being discussed behind his back, leaves briefly, only to overhear his two associates commenting on the relative lengths of his hind legs and his forelegs. Returning, he glares at the lion, who has indicated his dislike for being stared at. In the subsequent uproar, embers from the vulture's cooking fire are scattered and burn away the vulture's crest, for which he has asked respect. The narrative thus serves as a double *pourquoi:* it explains at once why these three meat eaters do not eat in company and why the vulture is bald. Still, the basic truth of Courlander's tale lies securely within the moral drawn by Olawale Idewu.

Three Friends and a Treasure

Volume 9 of Frobenius's *Atlantis* (pp. 133–34) affords a lively variant of this tale, made satisfactorily dramatic by the strategic use of dialogue. Titled "Bestrafte Goldgier," the spare German version—shared by the Nupe and by the Yoruba—presents three sisters determined to reach a certain hill to find gold. Although warned first by a toad and then by an old woman that if they find gold, they will also find death, the three persist, and they do indeed find not only gold but silver. As in Idewu's version, the youngest is beaten to death by the older two, who are in turn destroyed by the poisoned food, in this instance eaten after they have reported to their father the youngest's death by snakebite. As the sisters are being buried, both the toad and the old woman pass by, and each comments that the sisters had been warned about the probable consequence of their quest. Both versions contain warnings of death as a consequence of greed for gold, but only in Idewu's telling are there moral reservations concerning the committing of murder. Whether or not this probing of conscience is a matter of acculturation is open to question.

The Tortoise and the Boar [Boa]
The Tortoise and the Snake

With the replacement of "boa" for "boar" in the first of these two tales, the fact that the two narratives are basically one becomes obvious. In both of the versions (the first furnished by Idewu and the second by Adu), the snake (or boa) tires of dining with the tortoise and assumes the initiative in terminating their relationship.

A French-language translation of a similar Yoruba tale, found in Trautmann's *La Littérature Populaire à la Côte des Esclaves* (pp. 34–35), differs from the two stateside-collected tales in presenting the tortoise as the first to prove an ungracious host, with no motive other than that of playing a shabby practical joke. After having invited the serpent to lunch, the tortoise places himself on the dish of food so that his carapace completely covers the meal. When the serpent asks how he is to eat, the mischievous tortoise neither moves nor answers, and the serpent goes out greatly troubled. A few days later, the tortoise, accepting the serpent's invitation to dinner, finds his host coiled upon the dish of food so that it is inaccessible. To the tortoise's inquiry as to how he is to eat when the serpent has put a cover on the dish, the serpent observes that he is merely returning the kind of action the tortoise had taken toward him "the other day." Both the moral appended to Trautmann's tale ("Do not do to your friends what you would not want them to do to you") and the expression "breakfasted and dined," occurring early in the tale, might be attributed either to acculturation or to an effort on the part of the translator to carry the Yoruba original into French in a fashion meaningful to his readers.

134

Courlander's variant, "How Ijapa, Who Was Short, Became Long," found in his *Olode the Hunter* (pp. 37–39), closely parallels the versions provided by Olawale Idewu and Omotayo Adu in presenting the boa as the first to prohibit his guest's access to the food, in Tortoise's utilizing the device of a grass tail to duplicate the boa's ample coils, and in the closing exchange: When Boa asks how it happens that Tortoise was once short but is now long, Tortoise replies, "One person learns from another about such things." A detail inserted in Courlander's version to allow time for the false hosts' successive encirclements of the foods is noteworthy: in each instance, this positioning is accomplished while the guest has gone outside to wash before eating. Also, Courlander presents Tortoise as stopping at Boa's to eat en route home from a journey; there is no suggestion either of a practical joke or of the desire of a friend to terminate the sharing of meals.

Envy Can Kill

Three Yoruba variants affirm the continued presence of this tale in the oral tradition: Volume 10 of Frobenius's *Atlantis* furnishes a lengthy version (pp. 224–32) titled "Orisas Gabe"; Ellis's *The Yoruba-Speaking Peoples* in an untitled tale (pp. 244–49) provides the closest of the three to Idewu's narrative; LaPin in Volume 2 of her Ph.D. dissertation (pp. 361–68) includes a related tale currently told among the Yoruba, "The Senior Wife's Cooking Spoon."

In the first two variants cited, both the initial encounter of the hero (or heroine) and the subsequent meetings of the anti-heroines with the gift-givers occur—as in the Idewu narrative—at the marketplace. In each of these two variants, as in the Idewu tale, the mother of the anti-heroine refuses to accept the proffered portion of the hero's (or heroine's) gains, preferring instead to gain much more through her own daughter's imitation of the successful one. In both of these versions, also, various obstacles, in addition to those in Idewu's narrative—the Tree of Heaven and the Gate of Heaven in "Orisas Gabe," and "yon gloomy forest" and "yon craggy mountain" in Ellis's tale—lie along the way and are overcome both by the heroic figures and by the anti-heroic ones. In both the Frobenius and the Ellis tellings, the hero or heroine is set tasks (three in Frobenius's and two in Ellis's) and performs them successfully; the anti-heroines in both tales follow the gift-givers' instructions literally—but they fail to sense and do the *right* things. In both of these variants, as well, the hero or heroine chooses the silent calabashes and finds in them rich rewards; the anti-heroines, violating the gift-givers' advice, choose the speaking calabashes and reap well-deserved disaster from their contents.

Several other interesting features must be noted in these two variants: Though in Ellis's version the product hawked is palm oil, in Frobenius's variant the product is a hoe; in Ellis's story, the anti-heroine conceals a coin and claims she has received insufficient payment, and in the Frobenius form the anti-heroine refuses entirely to accept payment at the marketplace, determined instead to obtain the richer rewards available at the gift-giver's house. In Frobenius's tale, the gift-giver is an orisha, a member of the Yoruba pantheon; in Ellis's version, the gift-giver is a goblin (or a ghost, as in Idewu's telling). In Frobenius, the anti-heroine's third calabash yields a leopard, which kills her; in Ellis, the anti-heroine never opens the third calabash, for the deaf person inside her house cannot hear her cry for admittance—she is destroyed on the threshold

by the wild beasts contained in the second forbidden calabash. An indication of the importance of drumming in
Yoruba life and culture is shown in Frobenius's version:
the hero's second calabash yields a drummer; the anti-heroine's second calabash produces a one-eyed slave with a
drum.

In neither of these two variants is there evidence of "acculturation" in terms of objects or situations included; the
translation by Ellis does reveal an other-than-Yoruba
hand—"eat" for "ate," "yon," "the cowry that was want-
ing," and the end-rhymes in the song (". . . turn back/
. . . leave the track") and inversions of word order making such rhyming possible. End-rhyming is not present in
the Yoruba-language versions of the songs in a *cante fable*
(at least, in those that we have had the opportunity to ex-
amine); the presence of end-rhyming in the translations is
less a matter of acculturation, we feel, than it is a matter
of style. In a sense, it misrepresents the indigenous form
of the song—often enriched by internal rhymes and by
puns and other kinds of word play—but it does suggest
the appeal of sound to the listeners; repetition of the songs
and of the events (a source of delight to Yoruba audiences)
is more marked in the Frobenius version than in that of
Ellis, but both are more complete in that respect than are
most other published versions of Nigerian tales, including
the Idewu form.

LaPin's tale is included with the present set because—
although it involves cowives rather than the children of
cowives and although there are no obstacles to overcome
and no traveling companion other than the river that carries first the junior wife and then the bitterly envious senior wife to the place where the gifts are to be given—it
illustrates vividly the high cost of jealousy in a polygynous
household. In brief, the senior wife's cooking spoon is car-

137

ried away by the river while the junior wife is washing the utensils; sent by the senior wife to bring back her "spoon that makes every soup taste sweet," the junior wife returns "seven days" later laden with elegant gifts and furnished with the lost cooking spoon. The senior wife, contemptuously refusing her half of the treasure proffered, follows the same course, despite the evident resistance of the river, and returns with a load that she refuses to share with the junior wife; in the load, opened in the privacy of her locked room, are vipers, pythons, and a leopard that destroy her.

All four of these tales serve an important function in the culture out of which they have grown: they impress upon the listeners the need of harmony among cowives and their families and the tragedy that follows the rupture of such harmony by jealousy.

The Tortoise and the Tug of War

Among the rich range of Yoruba variants for this "chestnut" we have confined ourselves to two: "Erin and Erinomi (The Land- and Water-Elephants)," found in Ogumefu's *Yoruba Legends* (pp. 71–72), and "The Elephant and the Rhinoceros," from Baumann's *Ajapa the Tortoise* (pp. 117–20). The choice of this pair has been made because it demonstrates clearly the opposite poles of second-language handling of a single well-known basic tale.

Ogumefu's version bears marks of retelling rather than of translation from a dramatic oral version—"Tortoise was always fond of making mischief between harmless people" and "by this time he was, you may be sure, very far away"—but its effective use of dialogue makes this telling a valid one. An interesting twist in both Ogumefu's version and Baumann's (apparently drawn from a single source) is Tortoise's use of the term "weakling" to intensify each animal's resentment of the other: Tortoise tells Elephant that Hippo has called him [Elephant] a weakling; likewise, he tells Hippo that Elephant has called him [Hippo] a weakling. This provocation is sufficient to initiate the familiar tug of war; the combatants' discovery of Tortoise's cheat leaves them both "snorting with anger." There is no attempt by Ogumefu to treat this tale as a *pourquoi*.

Baumann's version is an overblown elaboration of the basic tale offered by Ogumefu, expanded by Tortoise's becoming annoyed at the refusal of both the elephant and the rhinoceros to return his greeting. Tortoise gains his revenge for this slight by confiding to each large animal the "fact" that the other had termed him a weakling. The dialogue used in this variant is chatty and includes a reminder of the "greeting" oversight as well as the challenge to demonstrate strength. Baumann's concluding paragraph transforms her version into a *pourquoi* (for which no preparation has been made in the telling): "They set off at once to look for Tortoise, but you may be sure he was nowhere to be found, *and to this very hour, he is still keeping out of their way*" [emphasis ours]. In general, Baumann's restyling of Yoruba tales misrepresents the very qualities that have kept such tales alive in the oral tradition. Her volume serves as an important tool in the analysis of use and abuse of oral materials.

The Elephant and the Tortoise

Three quite different Yoruba variants of the tale told by Omotayo Adu have been chosen for comment: Verse

139

SUPPLEMENTARY NOTES

222–1 in Bascom's *Ifa Divination* (pp. 450–53), "Der Elefant als Opfer auf dem Königsgrab" in Volume 10 of Frobenius's *Atlantis* (pp. 289–92), and "Jomo, 'Guardian of the Great Sword' " in Volume 2 of LaPin's dissertation (pp. 161–78).

As is true of all the narratives included in Bascom's *Ifa Divination,* this variant is intimately related to the practice of sacrifice among members of the Ifa cult. In this tale, two diviners tell the people of a certain town that they must sacrifice an elephant "for the good of their town" following the death of their king. Many hunters try to capture the required elephant, but all fail, whereupon Tortoise takes good foods and entices Elephant to the town, saying, "These are the things that you, Elephant, will be eating if you come home so that they can make you king. . . ." Elephant follows Tortoise to the town, where all the people cheer his arrival. Tortoise leads Elephant to a royal mat that, Tortoise says, is to serve as his throne; the mat has been laid over a pitfall, and thus the people gain their elephant for the sacrifice. In keeping with the sacred nature of its purpose, the tale is spare in the telling: there is no bird to warn Elephant; only a two-line song is sung, consisting of one line followed by another repeating it exactly ("We will take Elephant and make him king, Shekurebele"—Bascom notes that *"Shekurebele"* has no meaning but is added "to make the song sound sweet"); no anxiety or doubt is shown by Elephant throughout the tale; and there is no debate involved. Bascom's version thus provides a sound example of the way in which the essential features of many Yoruba tales have been preserved, whatever might or might not have been made of those same tales by other storytellers.

Frobenius's version provides both an introduction and a conclusion that differ significantly from those afforded in

140

other texts: the townspeople seek an elephant so that his
blood may be poured as a tribute over the grave of their
beloved deceased king; following this tribute, accomplished through the cleverness of the tortoise, the townspeople thank the tortoise and present him with a "scarf "
["cloth"?] which "never becomes old and is still good."
Many colorful details—all relevant—are furnished by
Frobenius, and there is highly effective use of dialogue.
Again, no bird appears to warn the elephant, and he goes
dancing to his death. In this variant, Frobenius unquestionably captures the spirit and drama of Yoruba oral
narrative.

A squinting parallel to Adu's tale appears as a significant portion of LaPin's "Jomo, 'Guardian of the Great
Sword.' " There is no elephant involved in this version,
nor is there a tortoise; instead, there is a powerful and
egotistical warrior, Jomo, whom the townspeople resent
and resolve to destroy. They consult Orunmila [Ifa, the
God of Divination], who advises them to dig a pit where
Jomo normally sits as "chairman" of the council meetings,
lay across it an "imported" mat, and make certain that
Jomo seat himself on the mat. A pit is accordingly dug and
covered with the mat, awaiting the arrival of Jomo from
battle. Meanwhile, Jomo's mother, who had died "about
twenty years earlier," changes herself into a bird and goes
to meet Jomo. Having heard the plans of the townspeople,
she repeatedly sings a song of warning (the song is furnished), urging him to throw a piece of pounded yam onto
the mat and send his dog to fetch the yam; in that way, the
deception can be revealed without harm to Jomo. But
Jomo does not hear the song, and continues his march toward home unaware of the plot against him. Jomo's
friend, "Wise One," says, "Take the *agiisasa* feather out
of your ear!" Jomo removes the feather, hears his mother's

song—interpreted by "Wise One"—replaces the feather in his ear, and determines to follow his mother's instructions. On the day of the council meeting, Jomo takes his own stool and sets it down in another place, refusing to sit on the mat provided for him. After he has dipped a piece of yam in the soup, he throws it onto the mat, and the dog, seeking the yam, drops into the pitfall prepared for Jomo. Jomo, enraged, is deterred from taking terrible revenge ("he would kill a thousand persons") by the timely counsel of an elder. From that point onward, LaPin's tale has no relevance to the present study, but the portion summarized serves to validate the association made in the oral tradition (as in Adu's story) between a bird as informer and the use of a disguised pitfall to gain a given end. The elements of the deceased's return in aid of a family member, of the bird as informer, and of the conspiracy of townspeople against a king or chief continue to be staples in Yoruba oral narrative.

The Girl Who Knew the King

The closest published Yoruba variant we have found for this tale told by Omotayo Adu is "Tintinyin and the Unknown King of the Spirit World," from Fuja's *Fourteen Hundred Cowries* (pp. 115–18). Tintinyin, orphaned, grows up "alone and uncared for" in the bush, befriended by the wild animals and birds, whose language he comes to understand "as well as he [understands] Yoruba." Every year, Tintinyin leaves the bush to participate in the great annual festival in the nearby town, a festival that the unknown king of the Spirit World is said to attend, unrecognizable because he always comes dressed as "an ordinary citizen." The powerful *oba* of the town, eager to see this mysterious figure, sends his bellmen out to find someone who will identify this special visitor and point him out to the *oba*. Success in identifying the unknown king of the Spirit World will be richly rewarded; failure will result in the luckless volunteer's being offered as a sacrifice to the sacred visitor. Tintinyin, confident that one or another of his bush friends will assist him, rashly claims that he can identify the visitor the *oba* seeks, but unfortunately no hints are offered by either bird or beast. At the crucial moment, Tintinyin's dead father, appearing as a small ega bird, sings a song reproaching Tintinyin for his boldness but saying, "I will not let you die." In his song, understood only by Tintinyin, he indicates the location and the tattered appearance of the unknown king of the Spirit World, a figure leaning on a staff. When Tintinyin points out to the *oba* the figure he seeks, the unknown king of the Spirit World reveals his symbol, the "tiny bead tied to a band around his ankle," and then he disappears. Tintinyin is duly rewarded and subsequently "[becomes] a rich and powerful man."

Fuja's handling of this tale seems to us somewhat "literary" and self-conscious, but the primary elements in the narrative are common to a number of Yoruba tales, and the song sung contains no end-rhymed lines, reflecting a pattern acceptable in the *alo* tradition.

The Body in the Coffin

Itayemi and Gurrey offer in their *Folk Tales and Fables* (pp. 86–87) a satisfactorily close Yoruba variant for this tale, "Tortoise and the Stolen Yams." In the variant, Tortoise, with no food of his own, finds a farm with many yams. Determined to take the yams home but reluctant to be identified as a thief, he settles on a clever trick: he takes a coffin to the farm, fills it with yams, and carries the load home. As he meets people along the way, he weeps and sings that seven people have been killed by a falling tree and that "he, unlucky he," has been left to carry each of the bodies home. His kind act earns him praise and sympathy, but his refusal of help in this morbid duty eventually prompts suspicion about the matter. After Tortoise's fifth trip, "some people [decide] to get to the bottom of it." Tortoise refuses to put down the coffin and allow them to see the face of the corpse, so before the seventh and last of Tortoise's trips they arrange to test the truth of this known trickster's claim. Smearing with pounded *okro* the small slope near the town gate through which Tortoise has carried the previous corpses, they wait to see what the coffin will reveal when Tortoise slips; "for fear of violating a dead man," they dare not open the lid of the coffin themselves. When Tortoise, "wailing as usual," slips on the *okro,* the yams fall out of the coffin, and Tortoise's deception is at once made apparent. Angry not only because of Tortoise's theft but also because of the dishonorable way in which he has concealed the stolen goods, "the people" beat him thoroughly.

Evidence that songs constituted a large portion of the oral version is afforded within the printed form: "Whenever he met anyone on the way he burst into tears and started to sing that a tree . . ."; with the repetition customary in Yoruba *cante fables,* such a song would have been sung at least two or three times for each of the seven trips Tortoise made from the farm to the town with the coffin. In this variant—really more a summary of a tale than a recreation of it—Itayemi and Gurrey have furnished neither songs nor dialogue, in effect weakening both the form and the force of what was quite clearly an *alo.*

The Promise

Three published Yoruba variants for the tale furnished by Omotayo Adu have proven helpful to us in assessing the degree to which essentially oral Yoruba folktales have been altered for accommodation to readers: "A Foolish Vow That Was Not Kept," in Itayemi and Gurrey's *Folk Tales and Fables* (pp. 33–34); "Oluronbi," in Ogumefu's *Yoruba Legends* (pp. 43–45); and "Oluronbi's Promise," in Baumann's *Ajapa the Tortoise* (pp. 88–95). In addition, we wish to call attention to a relatively recent variant of the Moremi legend (cited in the Notes for the first edition of *Nigerian Folk Tales*) included as "Moremi and the Egunguns" in Courlander's *Tales of Yoruba Gods and Heroes* (pp. 60–65). In Courlander's account, Moremi makes no attempt to substitute lesser sacrifices for the beloved son she had pledged to the sacred brook Esinminrin: as soon as Ife has been relieved of the terrifying attacks by the Egunguns of Ile-Igbo, Moremi takes her son Olu-Orogbo to the brook and gives him up, a sacrifice honored both by her townspeople and by Olorun, the Sky God.

Of the variants of Adu's tale itself, two (those by Ogumefu and by Baumann) concern promises made to the spirit of the *iroko* tree by childless women seeking to conceive, and the third deals with the promises made by women wishing exceptionally good prices for their wares in the marketplace; all these goals are to be achieved through the intercession of the *iroko* spirit. In Itayemi and Gurrey's variant, one of the women—Oluronbi, "a widow"—pledges her beautiful fair-skinned daughter, while the rest of the women pledge fowls, goats, or sheep; in the other two versions, Oluronbi pledges her first child, while the others promise corn, yams, fruit, goats, or sheep. In all three versions, Oluronbi, though most boun-

145

tifully blessed, fails to give the *iroko* spirit the child she has pledged as a sacrifice; all the other women meet their vows and have no trouble with the *iroko* spirit.

In all three variants, the bulk of the tale is concerned with the heavy price paid by Oluronbi for neglecting her vow. In the Itayemi and Gurrey version, the "dreaded" *iroko* spirit eventually demands "its due," refuses all substitutes, and takes Oluronbi's beautiful yellow-skinned daughter inside the *iroko* tree, from which she never returns. In the other two versions, Oluronbi herself, walking near the *iroko* tree, is snatched by the *iroko* spirit and changed into a small brown bird that sings a song about the promises that had been made. In both of these versions, Oluronbi's husband, a woodcarver, realizing that the bird must be his lost wife, carves a convincing life-size image of a beautiful child, dresses it richly, and offers it to the *iroko* spirit as the promised child; the *iroko* tree snatches the "child," and the small bird immediately becomes Oluronbi.

The narrative styles and the specific details offered in the three variants are quite different from one another despite their basic similarity in theme: the cultural imperative of keeping a sacred vow, a theme verbalized in the conclusion of the Itayemi and Gurrey version and mentioned in the latter part of the Baumann retelling. Songs are either described or furnished in all three variants: Itayemi and Gurrey's tale recounts the "dreaded" *iroko* spirit's singing of Oluronbi's unkept vow as the spirit comes through the town in search of the girl; Ogumefu's tale has the small brown bird sing a four-line unrhymed song describing the promises made; Baumann's retelling furnishes three songs, a two-line praise song sung by Oluronbi about her beautiful child, a seven-line song (with the last three lines end-rhymed) sung by the small brown bird relating both the promises made and the transformation of Oluronbi, and a seven-line song (with the last two lines end-rhymed) sung by the woodcarver offering the "child" to the *iroko* spirit and asking that the bird be set free. The Itayemi and Gurrey version appears the most distinctive and dramatic of the three in content: the blessing sought (the sale of market wares at a good price), the terrifying pursuit of Oluronbi by the singing spirit, the pathos of Oluronbi's pleas, and the finality of the widow's loss suggest that the oral version must have been a powerful warning to those inclined to make vows lightly. Ogumefu's version is at once brief and rather condescending in style, with little suggestion of the strength of an oral telling. The concluding sentence indicates the bland character of the whole: "Oluronbi joyfully returned home, and was careful never to stray into the forest again." Baumann's retelling is much longer than the other two, is heavily oversentimentalized, and includes much peripheral material (a meeting of the village men in which they consider driving the women into the bush because of their "fourteen years" of failure to bear children, descriptions of the woodcarver's elegant carvings, the eavesdropping of one of the women as the woodcarver promises to be the first to cast off his wife if the men will only wait one more year before taking such drastic action, the assurance that the king's son will wed Oluronbi's daughter, and the "lived happily ever after" ending as a consequence of the royal marriage) distracting the reader from the main point of the tale. Taken together, these three variants demonstrate vividly both the uses and abuses of oral narrative by those attempting to commit it to print.

Bibliography

Aarne, Antti, and Stith Thompson. *The Types of the Folktale: A Classification and Bibliography*. Folklore Fellows Communications No. 184, 2d rev. Helsinki: Suomalainen Tiedeakatemia, 1961.

Arewa, E. Ojo. "A Classification of the Folktales of the Northern East African Cattle Area by Types." Ph.D. dissertation, University of California (Berkeley), 1966. [Xeroxed copy available through University Microfilms, Ann Arbor, Michigan]

Arnott, Kathleen. *African Myths and Legends*. Oxford: Oxford University Press, 1962. New York: Walck, 1963. Reprint. Oxford: Oxford University Press, 1978.

Asamani, J. O. *Index Africanus*. Stanford: Hoover Institution Press, 1975.

Barker, William H., and Cecilia Sinclair. *West African Folk-Tales*. London: Harrap & Co., 1917; London: Sheldon Press [1928]; Northbrook, Illinois: Metro Books, 1972.

Bascom, William R. *African Dilemma Tales*. The Hague: Mouton, 1975.

———. "Folklore and Literature." In *The African World: A Survey of Social Research*, edited for the African Studies Association by Robert A. Lystad. New York: Praeger, 1965.

———. "The Forms of Folklore: Prose Narratives." *Journal of American Folklore* 78 (1965):3–20.

———. "Four Functions of Folklore." *Journal of American Folklore* 67 (1954):333–49.

———. *Ifa Divination: Communication Between Gods and Men in West Africa*. Bloomington: Indiana University Press, 1969.

———. "Verbal Art." *Journal of American Folklore* 68 (1955): 245–52.

149

BIBLIOGRAPHY

————. *The Yoruba of Southwestern Nigeria.* New York: Holt, Rinehart & Winston, 1969.

Basden, George T. *Among the Ibos of Southern Nigeria.* London: Seeley Service, 1921. Reprint. London: Frank Cass, 1966; New York: Barnes & Noble, 1966.

————. *Niger Ibos: A Description of the Primitive Life, Customs and Animistic Beliefs, &c., of the Ibo People of Nigeria by One Who, for Thirty-Five Years, Enjoyed the Privilege of Their Intimate Confidence and Friendship.* London: Seeley Service, 1938. Reprint. London: Frank Cass, 1966.

Basset, René. *Contes Populaires d'Afrique.* Paris: E. Guilmoto, 1903.

Baumann, Margaret I. *Ajapa the Tortoise: A Book of Nigerian Fairy Tales.* London: A. & C. Black, 1929.

Bellon, I. "Märchen des Tschi-Volkes auf der Goldküste." *Mitteilungen des Seminars für Orientalische Sprachen* 17 (1914):20ff.

Ben-Amos, Dan. "Introduction: Folklore in African Society." In *Forms of Folklore in Africa: Narrative, Poetic, Gnomic, Dramatic,* edited by Bernth Lindfors. Austin: University of Texas Press, 1977. [Published initially as "Folklore in African Society." *Research in African Literatures* 6 (1975):165–98.]

Bérenger-Féraud, Laurent J. *Recueil de Contes Populaires de la Sénégambie.* Paris: Ernest Leroux, 1885. Reprint. New York: AMS Press, 1980.

Bergsma, Harold and Ruth. *Tales Tiv Tell.* Ibadan: Oxford University Press, 1969.

Bettelheim, Bruno. *The Uses of Enchantment: The Meaning and Importance of Fairy Tales.* New York: Knopf, 1976.

Boas, Franz, and C. Kamba Simango. "Tales and Proverbs of the Vandau of Portuguese South Africa." *Journal of American Folklore* 35 (1922):151–204.

Boggs, Ralph. "North Carolina White Folktales and Riddles." *Journal of American Folklore* 47 (1934):289–328.

Bradbury, R. E. *The Benin Kingdom and the Edo-Speaking Peoples of South-Western Nigeria.* London: Oxford University Press, 1957.

Campbell, Robert. *A Pilgrimage to My Motherland: An Account of a Journey Among the Egbas and Yorubas of Central Africa in 1859–60.* New York: Thomas Hamilton, 1861.

Bibliography

Cendrars, Blaise. *The African Saga*. Translated by Margery Bianco from *L'Anthologie Nègre*. New York: Payson & Clarke Ltd., 1927. Reprint. New York: Negro Universities Press [1969].

Chase, Richard, comp. *American Folk Tales and Songs and Other Examples of English-American Tradition as Preserved in the Appalachian Mountains and Elsewhere in the United States*. New York: New American Library, 1956.

Clarke, Kenneth W. "A Motif-Index of the Folktales of Culture-Area V—West Africa." Ph.D. dissertation, Indiana University, 1958. [Xeroxed copy available through University Microfilms, Ann Arbor, Michigan]

Coughlan, Margaret N., comp. *Folklore from Africa to the United States: An Annotated Bibliography*. Washington, D.C.: Library of Congress, 1976.

Courlander, Harold. *The King's Drum and Other African Stories*. New York: Harcourt, Brace & World [1962].

————. *Terrapin's Pot of Sense*. New York: Holt, Rinehart & Winston, 1957.

————, comp. *A Treasury of African Folklore: The Oral Literature, Traditions, Myths, Legends, Epics, Tales, Recollections, Wisdom, Sayings, and Humor of Africa*. New York: Crown, 1975.

————. *A Treasury of Afro-American Folklore: The Oral Literature, Traditions, Recollections, Legends, Tales, Songs, Religious Beliefs, Customs, Sayings, and Humor of Peoples of African Descent in the Americas*. New York: Crown, 1976.

————, ed. *Tales of Yoruba Gods and Heroes*. New York: Crown, 1973.

————, and Ezekiel A. Eshugbayi. *Ijapa the Tortoise and Other Nigerian Tales*. London: Bodley Head, 1968.

————. *Olode the Hunter and Other Tales from Nigeria*. New York: Harcourt Brace Jovanovich, 1968.

————, and George Herzog. *The Cow-Tail Switch and Other West African Stories*. New York: Holt, Rinehart & Winston, 1947.

————, and Albert Kofi Prempeh. *The Hat-Shaking Dance and Other Tales from the Gold Coast* [subsequently retitled *The Hat-Shaking Dance and Other Ashanti Tales from Ghana*]. New York: Harcourt, Brace & Co., 1957.

151

BIBLIOGRAPHY

Crowley, Daniel J. "The Uses of African Verbal Art." *Journal of the Folklore Institute* 6 (1969):118–32.

Dayrell, Elphinstone. *Folk Stories from Southern Nigeria, West Africa.* London: Longmans, Green & Co., 1910. Reprint. New York: Negro Universities Press [1969].

Dennett, Richard E. *Nigerian Studies: or, The Religious and Political System of the Yoruba.* London: Macmillan & Co., 1910. New ed. London: Frank Cass, 1968.

Dorson, Richard, ed. *African Folklore* [including the papers read at the Conference on African Folklore, Indiana University, 16–18 July 1970]. Bloomington: Indiana University Press, 1972.

Echeruo, Michael J. C., and Emmanuel N. Obiechina. *Igbo Traditional Life, Culture and Literature.* Owerri, Nigeria: Conch Magazine Ltd., 1971. [*The Conch* 3 (1971).]

Edgar, Frank. *Hausa Tales and Traditions.* Translated by Neil Skinner from *Tatsuniyoyi na Hausa;* Hausa edition published 1911–13. Vol. 1. New York: Africana Publishing Corporation [1969].

Egudu, Romanus N. *The Calabash of Wisdom and Other Igbo Stories.* New York: NOK Publishers Ltd., 1973.

Ellis, Alfred B. *The Yoruba-Speaking Peoples of the Slave Coast of West Africa: Their Religion, Manners, Customs, Laws, Language, &c.* London: Chapman & Hall, 1894. Reprint. Chicago: Benin Press, 1964; Oosterhout, The Netherlands: Anthropological Publications, 1966; New York: Humanities Press, 1966.

Finnegan, Ruth. *Oral Literature in Africa.* London: Clarendon Press, 1970.

Forde, Daryll. *The Yoruba-Speaking Peoples of South-Western Nigeria.* London: International African Institute, 1951. [with Supplementary Bibliography through 1962]

————, and Gwilym I. Jones. *The Ibo and Ibibio-Speaking Peoples of South-Eastern Nigeria.* London: International Institute, 1950.

Frobenius, Leo. *Atlantis: Volksdichtung und Volksmärchen Afrikas.* Vols. 9 and 10. Jena: Eugen Diederichs, 1926.

————, and Douglas C. Fox. *African Genesis.* New York: Stackpole, 1937. Reprint. New York: Benjamin Blom, 1966.

Fuja, Abayomi. *Fourteen Hundred Cowries: Traditional Stories of the*

Yoruba. London: Oxford University Press, 1962; New York: Lothrop, Lee & Shepard [1971].

Gbadamosi, Bakare, and Ulli Beier. *Not Even God Is Ripe Enough: Yoruba Stories*. African Writers Series, no. 48. London: Heinemann, 1968.

Green, Margaret M. "The Unwritten Literature of the Igbo-Speaking People of South-Eastern Nigeria." *Bulletin of the School of Oriental and African Studies* (London) 12 (1948):838–46.

Hailey, Lord (Malcolm). *An African Survey: A Study of Problems Arising in Africa South of the Sahara*. London: Oxford University Press, 1936. Rev. ed. London: Oxford University Press, 1957.

Harris, J. Rendel. *The Cult of the Heavenly Twins*. Cambridge: Cambridge University Press, 1906.

Hartwig, Gerald W. *The Student Africanist's Handbook*. Cambridge, Massachusetts: Schenkman, 1974.

Herskovits, Melville J. "The African Cultural Background in the Modern Scene." In *Africa Today*, edited by C. Grove Haines. Baltimore: The Johns Hopkins Press, 1955.

————. "Tales in Pidgin English from Nigeria." *Journal of American Folklore* 44 (1931):448–67.

————, ed. "Bulu Tales Taken from the Collection of A. N. Krug." *Journal of American Folklore* 62 (1949):348–74.

————, and Frances S. Herskovits. *Dahomean Narrative: A Cross-Cultural Analysis*. Northwestern University African Studies, no. 1. Evanston: Northwestern University Press, 1958.

Hoffmann, C. "Märchen und Erzählungen der Eingeborenen in Nord-Transvaal." *Zeitschrift für Kolonialsprachen* 6 (1915–16): 28–54, 124–53, 206–43, 285–331.

Itayemi, Phebean, and Percival Gurrey. *Folk Tales and Fables*. London: Penguin Books, 1953.

Johnston, Hugh A. S., ed. and trans. *A Selection of Hausa Stories*. Oxford: Clarendon Press, 1966.

Kingsley, Mary H. *West African Studies*. London: Macmillan, 1899. 3d ed. London: Frank Cass, 1964.

Klipple, May Augusta. "African Tales with Foreign Analogues." 2 vols. Ph.D. dissertation, Indiana University, 1938. [Xeroxed copy available through University Microfilms, Ann Arbor,

BIBLIOGRAPHY

Michigan]

Krohn, Kaarle. *Mann und Fuchs: Drei Vergleichende Märchenstudien.* Helsingfors: J. C. Frenckell, 1891.

Lambrecht, Winifred. "A Tale Type Index for Central Africa." Ph.D. dissertation, University of California (Berkeley), 1967. [Xeroxed copy available through University Microfilms, Ann Arbor, Michigan]

LaPin, Deirdre. "Story, Medium and Masque: The Idea and Art of Yoruba Storytelling." 3 vols. Ph.D. dissertation, University of Wisconsin (Madison), 1977. [Xeroxed copy available through University Microfilms, Ann Arbor, Michigan]

Leach, Maria, ed. *The Standard Dictionary of Folklore: Mythology and Legend,* Vol. 1. New York: Funk & Wagnalls, 1949.

Lee, Frank H., ed. *Folk Tales of All Nations.* New York: Tudor Publishing Co. [copyright Coward McCann], 1930.

Leonard, Arthur G. *The Lower Niger and Its Tribes.* London: Macmillan, 1906. Reprint. London: Frank Cass, 1968.

Lindfors, Bernth, and Oyekan Owomoyela. *Yoruba Proverbs: Translation and Annotation.* Athens, Ohio: Center for International Studies, 1973.

Lüthi, Max. *Once Upon a Time: On the Nature of Fairy Tales.* Translated by Lee Chadeayne and Paul Gottwald from *Es War Einmal—Vom Wesen des Volksmärchens* (Göttingen: Vandenhoeck & Ruprecht, 1962). Bloomington: Indiana University Press, 1976.

Maris, Faith. *African Negro Folk Tales.* Little Blue Books, no. 807. Girard, Kansas: Haldeman-Julius Co. [1925].

Miller, Robert J. "Situation and Sequence in the Study of Folklore." *Journal of American Folklore* 65 (1952):29–48.

Mischlich, Adam. *Lehrbuch der Hausa-Sprache.* Berlin: Druck und Verlag von G. Reimer, 1911.

Ogumefu, M. I. *Tales of Tortoise.* London: Sheldon Press, 1932.

———. *Yoruba Legends.* London: Sheldon Press, 1929. Reprint. New York: AMS Press, 1980.

[These two original texts are now available in a single apparently abbreviated and somewhat confusing volume—carrying the title *Yoruba Legends* but including a number of Tortoise tales—

through University Microfilms, Ann Arbor, Michigan. Our notes refer to this Xeroxed volume.]

Okanlawon, Tunde. "The Narrator in the Nigerian Community." Unpublished paper read at the Seventh [quinquennial] Congress of the International Society for Folk-Narrative Research, Edinburgh, 12–18 August 1979.

Okeke, Uche. *Tales of Land of Death: Igbo Folk Tales*. New York: Doubleday (Zenith Books), 1971.

Olajubu, Oludare. "The Use of Yoruba Folktales as a Means of Moral Education." *Fabula* 19 (1978): 211–24.

――――. "The Yoruba Singers of Tales." Unpublished paper read at the Seventh [quinquennial] Congress of the International Society for Folk-Narrative Research, Edinburgh, 12–18 August 1979.

Parsons, Elsie Clews. *Folk-Lore of the Sea Islands, South Carolina*. Memoirs of the American Folk-Lore Society, 1923. Chicago: Afro-Am Press, 1969.

Paulme, Denise. "The Impossible Imitation in African Trickster Tales." Translated by Judith H. McDowell. In *Forms of Folklore in Africa: Narrative, Poetic, Gnomic, Dramatic*, edited by Bernth Lindfors. Austin: University of Texas Press, 1977.

p'Bitek, Okot. *Hare and Hornbill*. African Writers Series, no. 193. London: Heinemann, 1978.

Radin, Paul, ed. *African Folktales* [extracted from *African Folktales and Sculpture*, Bollingen Series 32, first published in 1952 and then in a revised edition in 1964]. [Princeton:] Princeton University Press, 1970.

Ross, Mabel H., and Barbara K. Walker. *"On Another Day . . .": Tales Told Among the Nkundo of Zaïre*. Hamden: Archon Books, 1979.

Saint-Andre-Utudjian, Eliane, comp. *A Bibliography of West African Life and Literature*. Waltham, Massachusetts: African Studies Association, 1977.

Scheub, Harold. *Bibliography of African Oral Narratives*. African Studies Occasional Paper, no. 3. Madison: University of Wisconsin, 1971.

Sidahome, Joseph E. *Stories of the Benin Empire*. London: Oxford University Press, 1964; Ibadan, Nigeria: Oxford University

155

BIBLIOGRAPHY

Press, 1967.

Stigand, Chauncey H., and Mrs. Chauncey H. *Black Tales for White Children*. New York: Houghton Mifflin, 1914.

Talbot, P. Amaury. *In the Shadow of the Bush*. London: Heinemann, 1912. Reprint. New York: Negro Universities Press, 1969; New York: AMS Press, 1980.

————. *Life in Southern Nigeria: The Magic, Beliefs, and Customs of the Ibibio Tribe*. London: Macmillan, 1923. Reprint. London: Frank Cass, 1967.

Thomas, Northcote W. *Anthropological Report on the Ibo-Speaking Peoples of Nigeria*. Vol. 3, Part 3: *Proverbs, Narratives, Vocabularies and Grammar*. London: Harrison & Sons, 1913. Reprint. New York: Negro Universities Press, 1969.

————. "Stories (Abstract) from the Anka Neighbourhood." *Man* 18 (1918): 23–25, 45–47, 56–57, 73–75, 84–87.

Thompson, Stith. *The Folktale*. New York: Dryden Press, 1946. Reprint. New York: AMS Press, 1977.

————. *Motif-Index of Folk Literature*. Rev. ed. 6 vols. Bloomington: Indiana University Press, 1955–58.

Trautmann, René. *La Littérature Populaire à la Côte des Esclaves*. Paris: Institut d'Ethnologie, 1927.

Travélé, Moussa. *Proverbes et Contes Bambara*. Paris: Librairie Orientaliste Paul Geuthner, 1923.

Tremearne, Arthur J. N. *Hausa Folk-Tales: The Hausa Text of the Stories in Hausa; Superstitions and Customs, in Folk-Lore, and in Other Publications*. London, 1914. Reprint. New York: AMS Press, 1980.

————. *Hausa Superstitions and Customs: An Introduction to the Folk-Lore and the Folk*. London: John Bale, Sons & Danielsson, 1913. Reprint. London: Frank Cass, 1970.

Umeasigbu, Rems Nna. *The Way We Lived*. African Writers Series, no. 61. London: Heinemann, 1969.

Vansina, Jan. *The Oral Tradition: A Study in Historical Methodology*. Chicago: Aldine, 1964.

Walker, Barbara K. *The Dancing Palm Tree and Other Nigerian Folktales* [retellings of Yoruba narratives gathered from Olawale Idewu]. New York: Parents' Magazine Press, 1964.

156

Bibliography

Werner, Alice. "African Mythology." In *The Mythology of All Races,*
Vol. 7. New York: Cooper Square Publishers, 1925, 1964.

Westermarck, Edward A. *The History of Human Marriage.* 3 vols.
London: Macmillan, 1921. Reprint. New York: Johnson Re-
prints, 1971.

Whiteley, Wilfred H. *A Selection of African Prose. 1. Traditional Oral
Texts.* Oxford: Clarendon Press, 1964.

Wonodi, Okogbule. "The Role of Folk Tales in African Society."
Africa Report, December 1965, pp. 17–18.